CANTONA

Other 442 books in Pan:

442: The Unofficial Biography of
LIVERPOOL by David Prole

FourFourTwo

CANTONA

RICHARD KURT

PAN BOOKS

To Veg, Zar, Streaker and
the Marx of Moreton Avenue
for all their support

First published 1996 by Pan Books
an imprint of Macmillan Publishers Ltd
25 Eccleston Place London SW1W 9NF
and Basingstoke

Associated companies throughout the world

ISBN 0 330 34975 9

9 8 7 6 5 4 3 2 1

A CIP catalogue record for this book is available from
the British Library.

Phototypeset by Intype London Ltd
Printed and bound in Great Britain by
Mackays of Chatham plc, Chatham Kent

Contents

CANTONA

Acknowledgements

Thanks to Paul Simpson & co. at *FourFourTwo*, 'Jim Morrison', Bill Campbell, Richard Milner, Graham Beech, Pete Boyle and above all the editors of *Red Issue*.

Particular thanks to the following who contributed to this book:
Jason Davies, Bernard Morlino, Mike B., 'Robbo', Andy Mitten, Steve Black, Melissa Moore, Dave S., Tony J., Jim White, Jamie Smith, Tony Graham, Jim Phelan, Peter Boyle and Mr Patrick Crerand.

About the author

Pseudonymous Richard Kurt is twenty-eight and as 'Red-Eye' contributes to every edition of the best-selling fanzine *Red Issue*. Educated at Manchester Grammar, Manchester University and Manchester United, he was brought up in Urmston's Red heartland. He gave up teaching European history to write books for fellow Reds, this being his fourth after *United We Stood*, *Despatches From Old Trafford* (both Sigma Press) and

As The Reds Go Marching On (Mainstream). He has also written for *The Independent*, *FourFourTwo*, *Total Football* and *The Game*. Having helped found the Independent Man Utd Supporters Association, the Eric The King Appreciation Society and the footie/pop group The K-Standers, he is now holed up amidst the enemy in Merseyside writing the story of United in the '70s.

Foreword

In the hours that followed the Cantona explosion at Selhurst Park, one Old Trafford legend stood firm and defended Eric wherever possible, inspiring Reds everywhere: Paddy Crerand. Outspoken, Red to the core and as much of a fighter as ever, he has arguably become the Reds' favourite warrior, not least because he speaks to the heart of the terraces. By the end of the 1994/5 season, Cantona and Crerand had become as inextricably linked as Boswell and Johnson. Here he reflects on the forging of a spiritual bond.

'I knew I was going to be taking a lone stand on Eric's outburst, at least for a while, but I wasn't bothered. As far as I was concerned he should never have been sent off in the first place. He'd had no protection from the referee and that sense of injustice was the root cause of what followed. I know how he felt – after all I've been there enough times myself! Such is the jealousy of United in the football world that the media reaction was, in some ways, predictable. But you put some people in front of a TV camera and they lose all rationality; so much of what was said about Eric was so hysterical, so lacking in intelligence, that you just have to shake your head in despair.

'You must understand that if you're a proud man with a keen sense of justice, these moments are hard on you: you're raging inside, you feel sick to the heart and you're bitterly disappointed for yourself and your team. That's something which Sir Matt fully appreciated. And that's why I think those people who claimed that Matt would've thrown Eric out were so wrong. Denis, George and I had our disciplinary troubles and Matt rightly gave us a bollocking and a hefty fine when necessary. But he also knew the position we were in, how difficult referees and opposition players make it for you. He understood players' temperaments and the pressure of the modern professional game; that's why I know he'd never have shown Eric the door.

'Besides, Eric is a real United player in the best traditions that Sir Matt established. I would love to have been able to play alongside him; he is a truly magnificent performer. It's his intelligence that appeals most of all; you don't need breakneck speed and muscle-bound power if you're visionary, clever and creative. Football today is full of fast, powerful players but there are situations that occur on the pitch which neither pace nor power will get you out of. Only intelligence will do it. Of course you've still got to be able to look after yourself – nobody else is going to be able to do it for you. Sometimes that'll get you into trouble, but there's no alternative.

'It's ironic that Eric has been portrayed as one of

football's "problems". There is so much more to find fault with in the football world: the authorities, refereeing standards, the media, our game's technical shortcomings. Eric is, I think, basically a nice, quite shy bloke who just wants to get on with his profession and be treated fairly. Every Red will hope that he is able to do just that for many years to come because what we have seen is unique – and I trust that Richard's book will provide ample illustration.'

Paddy Crerand

A Note to the Reader

Within the A to Z there are two subplots you might care to pursue by following the textual (>>) cross-reference signs. Eric's basic footballing career story starts with the Auxerre entry and runs to the climactic Venue Of Legends; if you're interested in following 'La Philosophie de Cantona', start at Jean Jacques Rousseau and follow through to Zodiac. The author would also like any PC types who object to the generalizations about the French herein to know that he himself is half-French and thus, on the Woody Allen/Jewish joke principle, invites you to get stuffed.

Introduction
The Making Of A Man

Old Trafford, February 1995. The visitors are Wrexham for an FA Cup tie but that is of secondary importance. We are all in the midst of the Cantona Wars and our stadium feels like a besieged castle. Inside, 40,000 roar Eric's name in defiance for ninety minutes. And although we are in the midst of crisis, the atmosphere is strangely euphoric. The struggle has brought us all closer together; for once, the many classes of Red are fighting for a common cause instead of squabbling amongst ourselves. We feel proud of each other; we have remembered why we are United. The spirit around Old Trafford is reminiscent of 1937 Barcelona, so thrillingly described by Orwell; had a banner proclaiming '*Seremos Invincibles!*' been strung across Sir Matt Busby Way, it would not have looked out of place. In a way, the history of the Cantonas had come full circle.

Catalonia, 1938. The Spanish Civil War is taking a turn for the worse. While the Axis powers use the struggle as a testing ground for their new weapons and tactics, granting Franco's Falangists a massive and murderous advantage, no number of idealistic International Brigade volunteers can compensate the Republicans for the disgusting indolence of Britain and France. Stalin meddles to little effect, encouraging only further divisions between the Republic's anarchists, communists and socialists; Barcelona will hold out for another year as an example of the truly egalitarian community before the dark forces finally triumph.

Pedro Raurich is thirty, a Republican officer freshly wounded while repelling a Fascist advance. There is no place for a retreat as behind-the-lines logistics are in chaos; monasteries and churches offer no sanctuary to a confirmed anti-cleric who knows that every cassock conceals a Francoist. The only option is a hazardous trek across the Pyrenees, young girlfriend in tow, to the relative safety of France. Paris may have been indifferent to the fate of Spanish democrats and the Catalan culture but at least in the Basque region that France shares with Spain, he would find help and solidarity. With Franco's final victory in 1939, there would be no way back: they would be waiting for him, gun in hand. Shunted from refugee centre to concentration camp and from there to Marseilles, eventual destination for every immigrant to the south, Pedro had become yet another in a generation of permanent exiles. His daughter, Eleanore, would be born a daughter of France but would inherit a burning Catalan pride.

There are a couple of north Mediterranean communities that can claim to possess the same toughness for which the Catalans are known: Corsica, once bizarrely cited by Rousseau (>>) as the ideal place to try his model of democracy; and Sardinia, whose inhabitants even the Sicilians treat with careful respect (lots of violin cases, if you get my drift). Ravaged by depression earlier in the century, Sardinians often chose Marseilles as an escape route rather than mainland Italy, where they would congregate in the Italian quarter around the Boulevard Oddo. There, away from the regionalist bigotries of Italy, hard-working immigrants and exiles could at least start to fight their way upwards in life on a level playing field; Marseilles is a cosmopolitan cross between Liverpool and New York, where the poor but proud can carve out an existence without sacrificing the culture of their ancestors.

Joseph Cantona, married to Lucienne, was one such Sardinian Marseillaise. And their son Albert, like Eleanore who was to become his wife, may have been born French but never lost the ferociously independent spirit that typified his family's native origins. Delving into the realms of genetics, blood-lines, culturally dictated behaviour and so forth is a dodgy business; many prefer to speak of the 'post-modern nomad' in which products of exile such as the Cantona boys have an entirely rootless identity. But as Stuart Hall argues in *Critical Dialogues*, although 'cultural identity is not fixed and is always hybrid, it does come out of a very specific historical formation'. Thus it is safe to say that this mix of Sardinian, Catalan and southern French cultural identities alone, leaving aside genetics and so-called 'blood-lines', was always likely to produce temperaments that are proud, fierce, independent and passionate.

Eric was born on 24 May 1966, the *annus mirabilis*

of Hurst hat-trick, 'El Beatle' Best and *Revolver*. But Swinging London was a world away from Cantona's environment. Not even the cat could swing in the tiny Cantona homestead, crammed in typical French style with three generations. The Cantonas were never well off. During the 1950s, the income from Joseph's stone-masonry had to be supplemented by Lucienne traipsing round the countryside selling a bit of this, buying a bit of that and consequently suffering the odd snobbish sneer of 'gypsy'. At least that gave her the opportunity to discover a home for the family in the summer of 1955. Remember that Python sketch where various old farts try to outdo each other with tales of childhood deprivation? At one point, one claims, 'we were a family of six and we had nowt but a hole in the ground to live in'. Eric wouldn't see what was funny about that; it's not far short of what passed for a habitation for the Cantonas: a cave, about ten foot by ten with a curtain instead of a door, high up in the hills of Caillols overlooking the city of Marseilles. Joseph spent the next decade carving a house around the cave, which not surprisingly became a minor tourist attraction for the city dwellers up there for a day out. Typically, Eric looked above the material to the spiritual dimension; the Marseillaises had to settle for one day's escape to the countryside per week. However proper their homes may have been, he was the one with the rural idyll outside his door, with a spectacular view over his entire world on permanent display. (Besides, having lived like prehistoric man must have been useful in empathizing with the Leeds Neanderthals in later life.)

Eric is the middle of three brothers; Jean-Marie is three years older, Joel eighteen months younger. Some would suggest Eric is a typical middle child, that touch more ambitious and demanding to compensate for being neither the first-born heir nor the little dauphin. There is little evidence, however, of fraternal rivalry for parental attention. The three Cantonas had a reputation in Caillols for being a tough band of brothers, fiercely loyal to family and their own individualism, classic exiles holding themselves together in a new land. All three shared a passion for football. From the age of three, Eric was always a regular in the street games, kicking Coca-Cola cans against garage doors before graduating to caseys; if not yet aware that Olympique Marseilles had just clinched their first modern honour in the 1969 Cup final, he was a *tifosi* in the making nonetheless. At six, he could understand and share in the region's jubilation as OM clinched a second successive title and made it a Double with the Cup in 1994 United style; months later, as he sat on his father's shoulders to watch the OM v. Ajax European Cup clash, he had his first true taste of football as gladiatorial theatre. He had glimpsed into his own future. Having long since abandoned the goalkeeping role his father had encouraged, he had now seen in Skoblar and Magnusson, the OM heroes, an ideal for which to aim.

If his father had done nothing else but inculcate his love for the game into his sons, that would be cause enough for gratitude. But as we shall see, that in itself would not have made Eric the special kind of player that he is. Albert, as a youngster in Gambert, had fallen for the beauty and spirituality of Provence, those magical qualities that have drawn artists and thinkers there for centuries; merely the experience of the unique Provence light is enough to ensnare most. His discoveries in turn led him to art, the only way open to him to express the feelings his surroundings had inspired in him. By regularly taking him into the countryside at dawn to hunt, explore and discover, and then by introducing him to the canvas and brushes in his workroom, Albert created the same opportunities for Eric to exploit. In doing so, Eric came to understand the true meaning of beauty and art as well as the joys of football; the way this combination of parental influences worked out has made him the unique player and man that he is. (>> Spontaneity, *Weltanschauung*)

It was in the aftermath of a Caillols boys' match that Albert taught Eric his single most important lesson. Like every kid on the street at that age, hogging the ball and dribbling with it until you fall over was his favoured *modus operandi*. There was an Algerian lad down the road who excelled at it; every other *gamin* tried to emulate his wizardry on the ball. Sure, Eric lionized the Dutch heroes whose defeat in 1974 had brought tears to his eyes but he was more in thrall to their individual play, not yet aware of the full team picture; the lessons taught by Platini were a few years away yet. So after Eric's team lost that night, the bollocking his father gave him for being too selfish and stupid with the ball was a stunner – but he never forgot his words. 'Make the ball do the work; look up before you receive it and pass rather than run. It goes quicker than you could ever carry it'. That moment, Eric now considers, marked the true beginning of his football apprenticeship.

As his development progressed to the point where he was outplaying lads four or five years older in Caillols boys' teams, the former international Celestin Oliver took him under his wing to take over his education from Albert; football became not only Eric's passion but his commitment, and a single-minded one at that. His scholastic education at Grande Bastide secondary took a back seat in consequence. His teachers didn't doubt his intelligence but his spirit was clearly elsewhere; there would be time for auto-didacticism later in life. The Cantona temperament developed apace too: there were frequent clashes with other kids, frenzied tantrums that smashed many a ping-pong bat when he lost at table tennis, and a formative experience of the pedantry of officialdom when a crucial title goal was denied because his bootlaces were undone. So he was going to be no easy-going, placid Platini; but for the scouts who were beginning to congregate around him at Caillols, it didn't matter. His passion and self-belief matched his precocity – this was one lad who wouldn't need motivation, just guidance.

Late spring, 1981. Eric is about to turn fifteen, now a tough strapping lad more man than child. He has been that most fortunate of men: to have had an idyllic childhood, to have been taught good values that will endure, and now to have a family offering support for whatever choices he makes. He has to decide whether Caillols has taught him as much as they can, and if so, should his destination now be Nice or Auxerre? No doubt as to which would be the easiest option: to stay put and cling to his youthful utopia a little longer, as any fifteen-year-old would be justified in choosing. 'The prospect of leaving my family made me cringe; it is only at the moment the door opens that one realizes how much one is attached to place, family and home.' And a second-best compromise would be to opt for Nice, the suggestion of Celestin and favoured by his family, which would allow him to come home as often as he liked and remain a semi-detached homestead dweller. But Eric was to choose the hardest, harshest alternative and did so by relying on his instinct; by his choice, which demonstrated an existential strength, and by his method, he demonstrated facets that are now recognized as typical of Eric the man. The rest of this book covers the adventures of the adult Cantona, but as we shall see, the spirit, experience and ancestry of the inner child have never been suppressed. (>> Auxerre)

'A' is for . . .

Anticipation

'**M**an cannot live on the bread of *schadenfreude* alone', as a wise man probably never said. Ten days of frenzied delirium following Eric's signing had encompassed a range of delighting in Sheep City's misfortune not witnessed since we completed our Trilogy Triumph back in January (>> Tony J, Jason Davies). If anything, this had surpassed all: instead of taking mere points and Cup places whose losses Elland Road overcame, we had snatched the very soul of 'New Leeds' and destroyed their future. By the night of 6 December 1992, however, our happy persecution of the woolly genitalled Tykes would have to cede precedence to the greatest issue of all – the Holy Grail. Yet again, there was a title summit visible; yet again we were in trouble in the foothills. Was Cantona really the path-finder to lead us out of the Valley of Death? However much we'd drunkenly revelled in this ten-day interlude of merriment in the pubs and papers, over airwaves and Pennines – and fun had been in short supply in 1992, so who could blame us? – the sober moments of reckoning awaited us on the pitch beneath the unforgiving glare of TV and floodlight.

He'd already transformed the team without yet stepping on to that illuminated battlefield. The mere knowledge that 'someone' was coming acted as a quid of baccy
up the horse's arse, the ageing nag himself scoring twice
against Oldham. And did Hughesie feel Eric's intense
studied glare in his bones at Highbury when he led the
line as of old, barging home the winner? There could
only be one upfront partner for Eric; had the 'Odd
Couple' of OT sensed what riches a future king might
bring to a warrior at his side?

Nah, 'course they hadn't. At the time both strikers
were often having trouble seeing what was coming at
them in the next few seconds let alone being able to
divine collective destinies months away. We were all
simply in a struggle for survival. Already out of two cups
and filleted twice by leaders Villa, we were off the pace,
often out of sorts and eight to one against with Lad-
brokes. When you're ten grand down at Vegas blackjack
and Robert Redford's not on hand to proffer a million
for your stretch-marked missus, you might as well stick
your house on the Red King comin' out the deck. One
Busbyesque trait that Fergie has acquired is the love of
a gamble, the willingness to tempt fate. Whereas Matt
high-rolled with the horses, Alex does it in the transfer
market, an even riskier game since unfortunately you
can't whip players, put blinkers on them or melt them
down for glue when they start buggering up. With Dion
in the stable and Hirst denied him, Alex put everything
on a man who may have been the purest thoroughbred
but who 'carried a whiff of sulphur' from a trail of
desertion, destruction and demoniac self-expressionism.

Or so the gutter press told us: good thing that Fergie reads the staid old *Express*. Whatever, he took the bet. In another phrase you'd recognize from the press, we were all – players, fans, Fergie and Eric – now drinking in the 'Last Chance Saloon'. (>> Arrival)

Arrival

To see a player who later becomes a hero make his debut is a special moment to treasure, much like the time you lose your virginity. Chances are the actual quality of the experience will only make your knees tremble rather than the earth, but the point is you've done it, you'll never forget it and you can only get better. However, for United fans going to watch new strikers there's an added anxiety. The 'Heartsearch' columns and porno shops are full of sex casualties who, after several disastrous initial attempts at planting the flag-pole, never recover and roam the earth with only the five-knuckle shuffle for company. So too do we at OT get an extravagant share of their footballing equivalents, the goal-mouth impotents who can't stick it in for the first three or four games and end up wilting altogether before leaving OT to the same bellowed description as befits their Soho-bound counterparts – 'w*nker!' In football's metaphorical red-light zone, you see them still: Brazil, Birtles, Super(dirty)mac, Wyn Davies . . . But from the start, this French cockerel stood too firm and proud ever to risk joining that Kleenex-clutching queue.

He probably didn't so intend it but Fergie did well to infiltrate Eric into the *Sturm und Drang* of a derby

for his debut. On a most Mancunian of nights, as pol-
luted rain pissed upon the pac-a-mac brigades in the new
Strettie, even the appearance of one such as Eric took
second place to the blood-feud on the pitch and in the
stands. Switching sex metaphors, this wasn't to be a
full striptease and twenty-quid 'special' from the new
performer – the stars tonight were the '92 stalwarts of
the Guv, Hughes and Giggs. This was more a case
of slipping in, giving the punter's packet a squeeze and
leaving a calling card with the promise of delights to
come. (Apologies for appearing to allude to Eric being
a bit girlie but then in some ways as a player he is more
in touch with what might be called a 'feminine side'
than any other. The reliance on intuition and instinct,
the ability to read and adapt to his own feelings, his
absolute selflessness in creating opportunity for the more
aggressive, less visionary 'macho' players . . . it's one of
the many dualisms in his nature (>> Zodiac).)

But when, only moments after the restart, he pulled
wide, made space and planted the most gorgeously
weighted defence-splitter into a surprised McClair's path,
he demonstrated exactly what he was about to bring to
us. Older heads in the stands might have recalled
Muhren, the luckier could summon up Paddy Crerand:
in short, we had a Creator again. ('Dieu' always was a
fitting appellation.) A minute later, he set up a Hughesie
header; when the Dragon fired his scorching winner, it
was Eric who'd lost his pursuers to hover at the edge of
the box, ready if needed for the follow-in. His time to
prove he could be a Destroyer as well as Creator would
come. And although Eric said his performance had been

'mediocre', Fergie now claims he himself was already convinced; and if any of us had ceased our rampant Bitter-baiting for a moment afterwards, we too could've testified to the beginnings of an outbreak of Francophilia. (>> Zapateado)

Authority

Authority: the response to the very word itself divides the world into conservatives, be they of left or right, and true libertarians. If its sound comforts you, conjuring up images of reassuring protective power, then you're the former; if it summons up visions of oppression and jackboots, you're the latter. You would expect a free-spirited existentialist rebel like Eric to be predisposed against everything bureaucratic; when you consider that he's been royally shafted in every confrontation with these bogus self-perpetuating élites, it's a wonder that he hasn't yet become a fully paid-up anarchist.

Round One. It's August 1988 and Eric has turned the corner at Olympique Marseille, man of the match in successive games. The outstanding star of the Under-21s, he's already broken through to the full national side and confidently awaits a call-up for the Parc des Princes clash with the Czechs. Instead, manager Henri Michel publicly declares that Eric's form is useless and Cantona is humiliated. Days later, trapped in a post-match tunnel TV interview, Eric opines that Michel 'is not far from becoming a *sac à merdes*'. The contents of that bag duly hit the fan. When people ask why Eric is so unapologetic now when he transgresses, they should remember that he tried the penitent route here and got absolutely nowhere. Recognizing that he had been 'clumsy', he immediately made a public apology and then tried to contact Michel to explain personally. His reward was a one-year international ban, which immediately ruled him out of a crucial World Cup qualifier against Cyprus in which he could surely have rescued France from an embarrassing draw. Moreover, he couldn't play in the final of the Under-21 Championship, a game he had done more than most to help France reach. If that's where public self-flagellation gets you, no wonder he felt disinclined to repeat it in 1995. The irony, as Cantona himself soon realized, was that his description of Michel had been spot on. If in August he had been 'close to becoming a shitbag', then by October he had indeed become the smelliest shitbag itself. When France slumped to Cyprus, Michel got the boot; it later transpired that his cards had been marked for some time. He was not Eric's idea of a purposeful leader: he'd capped fifty players in two years and seemed to sway with the hot and cold winds of the press farts. Yet in voicing a truth recognized by many, Eric had been labelled a criminal of football.

Round Two. In 1991 a minor altercation in the match between Nimes and St Etienne results in Eric throwing the ball towards the referee where it bounces harmlessly against his legs. Or, if you read the accounts in the Parisian press, Monsieur l'Arbitre is lucky to survive an assassination attempt that could have foreshadowed a Cantona *coup d'état*. Whatever: Eric is back in front of the League disciplinary committee, the judge, jury and executioner being Jacques Riolaci. In response to Eric

asking for reassurance that he'll get a fair hearing on the
merits of the case alone, Riolaci makes it shockingly clear
that Cantona is to be singled out. He gets a one-month
ban. Thankfully, videotape has preserved Eric's reply, to
be replayed with pleasure for years to come: to each
disciplinarian in turn, Eric hisses *'idiot!'* in their ear.
Undoubtedly one of the coolest Cantona moments yet
– the result is an extra month's ban. Anyone who's stood
in a dock when the judge asks if you have anything to
say and felt impelled to yell 'Yes, you're a corrupt, senile,
Mason-shagging twat', knows exactly how he felt. Still,
at least he could soon console himself with the thought
that in England, the bastion of fair play, he'd never get
such shabby treatment, right?

Round Three. Anglo-Saxon justice doesn't allow a
defendant to run the risk of double jeopardy. But quad-
ruple jeopardy? That's mandatory for them bastard
garlic-crunching Gallics. After Selhurst Park, the club
ban, if in retrospect mistaken, was understandably politically expedient; that the FFF should also be glad to join
the lynch-mob was sadly predictable too. Eric had ruffled
too many preening feathers while national captain with
his talk of 'pissing on critics' arses' to be able to expect
any favours. But you could have hoped for so much
more from the FA and the courts. Lancaster Gate had
always been a byword for cack-handed slackness, leniency
and indolence, so their comprehensive stitching-up of
United showed unwelcome and remarkable slyness. As
for the magistrates' court, what unpleasant flashbacks for
Eric – judged on who he is rather than what he'd done in
Riolacian manner by people from the same authoritarian

conservative class whose jurisdiction he thought he'd escaped when he fled the tribunals of Paris.

Such have been Eric's Kafkaesque experiences at the hands of authority; little surprise then that his own verdict is 'a legal system is not in a position to give lessons of virtue and morality to anybody'. Football's disciplinary system should be run by the players themselves, not by tinpot nobodies in blazers. And magistrates should be elected, not self-selected from the same cosy, bourgeois and largely Conservative-voting world of square-dealers and establishment lap-dogs. As the Cantona examples demonstrate, the greatest threat to the rule of law in both football and society does not come from the obvious critical assailants but from the unerring ability of these authorities to bring themselves into public disrepute quite unaided. (That was a Party Political Broadcast by the Cantonista Anarcho-Syndicalist Front.)

Auxerre

There can't be many international stars who've been 'transferred' on the strength of a free club shirt; it's reminiscent of those frequent stories you see in whimsical columns – wee Jock McTavish moves from Haggismolesters FC to their rivals Old Sporransniffers for three chocolate oranges and a set of Subbuteo nets. It seems remarkable that a lad just about to turn fifteen, wrestling with such a key, heart-wrenching decision, should have chosen Auxerre over Nice primarily because the Burgundians bunged him a few freebies from the club-shop hut. For Eric, the intellectual rationalizations came second:

as so often in his career, he let instinct and intuition guide him. That initial gesture had shown Eric that they were sensitive to his desires and needs; they – ugh – 'cared'. Everything else the budding player needed – a family atmosphere, good youth policies, careful personnel management – would surely follow from that first principle.

How right he was. At the first great crossroads of his life, he felt the contradictory pulls from two defining forces in his personality and heritage (>> 'Lodger', Family Values). By relying on his favourite principle of obeying the instinct of the inner child, this young man chose the turning north and headed towards the welcoming, avuncular figure of Guy Roux.

Roux is an eminently lovable creature, a one-club man since 1962, much revered for his principles and integrity throughout French football. Sat morosely in his dugout under one of his collection of silly woolly hats, he looks like a character from *Asterix*. The club, which survives on small gates drawn from a 40,000 population, has emerged to build a national reputation to challenge that of the local Chablis by inculcating a succession of youth-team graduates with the virtues of neat, cultured passing football. When Eric arrived, the club was achieving new highs – Cup finalists in '79 and into the First Division the following season. And from the beginning, Roux marked Eric out as a future international and the best of his group: he already had much of the skill and vision with only self-discipline yet to be acquired. A full-time professional contract would surely only be a matter of time.

In his lonely lodgings room, the uprooted outsider initially endured the existence of a Sartrean novel's narrator, racked by homesickness and existential angst. His escape was to define himself through his work, his art of football. Eric's precocity, matched by an ability to learn all that Auxerre had to teach, propelled him up the club pyramid. Within the year, he was regularly being thrown into practice matches with first-teamers, often humiliating those trundling old defenders who sought to teach the *petits gamins* a physical lesson or two. But at this family club, every nasty uncle like Lucien Denis had a cool cousin to counterbalance, one such being the Polish star Andrej Szarmach. A player of the utmost sophistication and class, his encouragement and role-model status appear to have made quite an impact on Eric. As ever, his heroes mattered to him: if the Pole was not exactly a Diego or Platini in Eric's eyes, he remained at least a tangible, contemporary touchstone for daily inspiration.

At sixteen, Eric was already in the Third XI and breaking through for occasional reserve matches, bamboozling lads two or three years older by virtue of a vision previously thought to be the preserve of those in their mid-twenties. His selection for the French schoolboys was a formality. And though contemporaries still thought him a touch withdrawn, the days of bedsit tears were behind him; he was now beginning to make some of the most important friends of his life, who remain with him today. (For the famous, the bonds forged when in anonymity must endure; once a celebrity, your acquaintances can rarely shake the soupçon of suspicion that inevitably

lingers and prevents them joining the 'old friends'.)
When, in the late summer of '83, Bernard 'Nino' Ferrer
arrived from Vichy, he catalysed a reaction in both Eric's
personal and professional life that set him irrevocably on
the long, winding road to Old Trafford.

That Nino had the most alluring, Cantona-compatible
sister was one thing (>> Isabelle); that he also comple-
mented Eric on the pitch so well was what mattered for
Auxerre's reserves. Bagging virtually a half-century of
goals between them, the duo led the side to the 1984
Third Division title; Eric's bonus was a couple of call-
ups to the firsts to play alongside Szarmach. Not even
the dreaded National Service call-up that dominated his
1984/5 season could dampen Eric's zest for life. Ending
up in a 'sports battalion' near Paris rather than potato
peeling in God-forsaken *outre-mer*, Eric and Nino
enjoyed a full-on *Loaded* lifestyle. It is said he emerged
still not knowing how to reassemble a rifle but fully
expert at the disassembly of France's vineyard products.
In retrospect, it was the last *grande bouffe* blow-out of
a teenager. Amidst all the debauchery, he still chiselled
further career milestones – his first Division One goal
against Rouen in May, soon followed by the equalizer
against Strasbourg that put Auxerre into Europe. But
within a year, 'maturity' had taken its grip as he signed
full professional terms for Auxerre and fell into a whirl-
pool of romance with Isabelle. 'Eric the lad' gave way
to Eric, *l'homme sérieux*. (>> *Bonjour Tristesse*)

'B' is for . . .

Bernard Morlino

A'journaliste littéraire', *Parisian Red, Pete Boyle fan and a favourite Cantona interviewer. As he tootles around the Place Charles Dullin, car stereo blasting 'Songs from the Bathtub' at startled passers-by, he dreams of his next trip to Old Trafford. (Thanks to B.T. for translating his high-flying French prose.)*

Certain footballers are more gifted than intelligent: others vice-versa. Cantona is both of these. How often have you seen him offside? Only the best in the League can ever defeat him. This player has the presence of one whom we know has something to say. However, it seems to me that he doesn't say all that he thinks but rather thinks about everything he says. He is the living embodiment of his sport, a mixture of spontaneity and anticipation, displaying both equally well in adversity. I like his vision of the game, his team spirit, his strength, concentration and elegance – even the tackles he makes that so enrage Ferguson. These tackles interest me for they are always executed under suicidal conditions, desperate and even dare we say naive, consequently child-like.

France is still asking itself if he has talent, whereas England celebrates his genius. His natural ability saps his worst enemies who fear him because he has the courage to display the man before the player. If France does not select him for Euro '96, his absence will be felt more than that of any other Frenchman. Let us not forget that France threw one of its best poets into the communal grave, namely Lautréamont. Cantona understands well the words of Chateaubriand: 'One must be economical with one's contempt – there are so many who are deserving of it.'

14 May 1994. Faced with two penalties, he displayed an Olympian calm that remains a reference point: a slow-action walk, preceding the eruption of the volcano. I also remember his body tricks, his strutting, the luminous overtures and of course his blinding willpower against Blackburn and Liverpool; on his comeback, he entered Old Trafford without even making the sign of the cross where others would have carried twenty bibles under each arm. I have only one regret for him: he will never be able to watch himself play live. I consider him one of my spiritual fathers, even though his age could only make him my son.

Bonjour Tristesse

. . . et adieu Auxerrois. The serious intent that becoming
a career footballer and prospective family man engenders
was always going to take him away from Auxerre at some
point. Guy Roux always knew it too: how often it had
happened to his illustrious children. Towards the end as
Eric's self-possession, so often dubbed arrogance,
increased alongside his ambition, contemporaries reflect
that the paternal Roux could neither hold nor control
his fidgety prodigy. Ian Ridley quotes Erik Bielderman
reckoning that Roux was by now 'afraid' of Eric, wondering where the next outburst of 'southern temperament'
might explode (>> Violence). Whatever, like any good
father whose child has needs he can no longer fulfil, he
allowed Eric to go elsewhere in pursuit of the new horizons Auxerre had helped him to visualize.

When the end did come, it was wonderfully Cantonesque. Back in autumn '85, a very different Eric had
accepted with equanimity his relegation from the firsts
due to Roger Boli's good form. Playing for Martigues
on loan for the rest of 1985/6 suited his new priorities:
Isabelle, Isabelle and Isabelle. To score four in sixteen
there was commendable, given how draining the shag-
fest of his first year alone with her must have been. But
upon his return to complete his first two full pro seasons
at Auxerre, the progression curves of club and player
began to diverge. Whilst Eric became France's dauphin
in both Under-21s and full national team, Auxerre had
apparently reached the glass ceiling that accounts for the
Norwiches of football. Without the resources to buy

stars to complement youth products, third or fourth place and a good Cup run seemed to be the summit of ambition. For a player who visualized himself on bedroom walls next to Platini, Maradona and Cruyff, a club who will never win in Europe or be cheered by 40,000 every week can never suffice. Nemesis with that Eric twist came at the hands of Lille in the 1988 French Cup quarter-finals. He took the defeat badly and decided there and then that the time to move had come. That the crunch should come because of a Cup defeat, rather than their League status, was telling. It is fashionable to laugh at European domestic cups but Eric, ever the romantic, always saw the magic of the knockout principle: glory or death in one fight, a stage set for heroic deeds. As a boy, he had thrilled to Marseilles's final triumphs in 1972 and 1976; once again, he had been denied this joy as a man because, as he saw it, of the club's lack of ambition.

Perhaps, subconsciously even, he saw that he was ready for a destiny of sorts. Eric doesn't believe in Fate, at least not in terms of a Heavenly Beard screenplaying your life story for you, so inevitability is not the right word for what transpired in the summer of '88. But throughout Eric's career thus far, the name of Olympique Marseilles had flashed subliminally, sometimes mentioned explicitly: l'OM, the club he supported as a boy, the magnet for Provençal talent, the one true and great footballing centre of the Midi. Eric had often suggested, half in fancy but betraying a deep desire nonetheless, that the time would come for him to 'go home'. Now aged twenty-two with over eighty first-class games behind him and a burgeoning international career ahead, he felt experienced enough to leave his first-class finishing school and take on the big-stage engagement. But Marseilles's dark side streets hide villains at every turn, and the biggest of them all awaited Eric at Olympique. (>> Olympique Marseilles)

The Bootroom

Sadly the Matthews-era days of playing on, fortified by Capstan Extras and half-time stout, until you're forty-seven are long gone; some time, soon after the turn of the millennium, the grim retirement reaper will come to claim Eric's Nikes. Thankfully, the fact that his game depends on vision rather than pace should mean he'll last longer than most, but the time is coming for Eric to consider his post-playing career. Will he retire to Provence and attempt to become a Cézanne for the new century? Or will he take the easy, parasitic Lineker/ Hansen route and become a mumbling media pundit?

Fortunately, the signs are that he can't remain immune to the intellectual challenge offered by coaching and management, at least judging by his 1995 appearance on Sky's *The Bootroom* with Andy Gray. Clearly, the man has studied his chosen art too much to throw it all away. Whilst Gray fawned and gawped at his side, unable to contain his excitement at netting the King for the show, Eric unveiled the sum of what he had learned in ten years of playing every kind of footballing system and presented his own prescriptions for success. For any United fan left scarred by European failure, Eric had a

vision for the future; what's more, the rumour of 1995/
6 has been that Ferguson himself is about to embrace
the Cantona perspective. These were his three steps to
heaven. Firstly, accept that the era of out-and-out wing-
ers is over. Reds bred on 4–2–4 variants would be hard
to wean away from the flying Andreis and Hills but Eric
is convinced that it's all too predictable. Away in Europe
especially, the fixed winger is easily isolated and leaves
the midfield too open; in general, they're an outdated
legacy from an over-structured, fixed-position mentality
age. Secondly, if you're going to stick to a 4–4–2 line-up
and want to combine the best of English and Continental
methodology, then go for a variant on the AC Milan
system. Eric introduced some highlights from his video
collection to illustrate how the modern midfield should
operate, as an integrated yet highly mobile tank unit,
compact rather than extended, each individual being
positionally flexible yet holding to an overall pattern.
When you compared what he demonstrated to how
United played in Gothenburg, you could only submit to
his logic.

But for Eric personally, if he had a club at his disposal,
the ultimate goal is a step further. His ideal is a mix of
Ajax, AC and United, nominally configured as a 5–2–3,
adaptable to a 3–4–3 but in fact a combination of Total
Football's freedom and fluidity with modern tight
internal structures. Tight but loose – the Stone Roses
paradox on a football field. He had no videos to demonstrate because it is, as yet, all in his head, but he spoke
with such dedicated enthusiasm that any football-lover
would pray he gets the chance to unfurl his plans in

reality. As he patiently outlined how each unit would move and support, how traditional labels and duties would be jettisoned and how opposing teams would be drawn into its traps, even such a traditional old barger like Gray seemed to fall under the spell. And if this is indeed United's future too, be prepared to be enchanted.

'C' is for . . .

Cantona Defence Campaign

It probably never existed, but they say that a couple of the death threats floating around after Selhurst Park were signed 'The CDC' (before any Sinn Fein/IRA-type connections are made, we at the Eric The King Appreciation Society believe in non-violent means, with the odd lapse when fifteen pints/Leeds neo-Nazis/'The Curryman' are involved). These days, the once shocking footie-related death threat is a matter of routine: linesmen now get them after dodgy offside decisions, stadium caterers for overcharging on a pizza pastie. Only the saddoes at *Football Monthly* still get their knickers soaked over them. Back in January '95 though, they were still a bit of a novelty: but they were the harshest testament yet to the extraordinary passions unleashed within the United brotherhood by the Cantona kick.

In the aftermath of Selhurst Park, the first twenty-four hours were the worst. The tabloid treatment, if amazing for its intensity, was nevertheless predictable in tone; what was more depressing was the sight of assorted lemmings and cretins claiming to be Reds who were prepared to diss the King on air. Who were these creatures, never seen before nor since? For a few hours, it appeared that only Paddy Crerand was out there fighting, under attack from ahead and behind. (Never fight a European land war on two fronts, as every German child would warn.) The symbolic nadir was a local TV sequence showing a mother trying to return an Eric shirt to the superstore to have the name removed. Who was the more disgusting, the treacherous and apparently half-witted harridan or the TV crew who had clearly set up the shot yet tried to pass it off as the *actualité*? Both parties typified the kind of attitudes we appeared to be up against; within days, however, the agenda had been seized back by loyal Reds.

From every quarter of the Red planet, the support for the King was overwhelming – the media soon ceased their attempts to portray us as split and instead resorted to panning us for our 'blind loyalty'. The fanzines, recognizing that this was precisely the sort of moment for which they were invented, led the line in best Hughesie fashion, pummelling dissenters into the ground, supplying us with ammunition for our pro-Eric arguments and exhorting all Red Army troops into action. The political wing, exemplified by *Red Attitude*, opened up the wider implications and introduced the kind of arguments with which many non-United left-leaners throughout the country felt impelled to agree. The Burnage Boy supervised the creation of the Eric The King Appreciation Society, whose mobile units travelled the nation to support the King wherever he appeared – most memorably at Croydon Magistrates and on *The Big Breakfast* – whilst their artistic division turned out songs, chants, press articles and letters in a constant flow of Cantona-worship.

As ever, United fans rescued a triumph of sorts from disaster. No Red who was active during those months could deny that the shared experience of embattlement brought us all closer together. It had been a chance to redefine one's Redness, to remind oneself of what being United means. The fact that this catastrophe had befallen Eric rather than another player probably doubled the fans' resolution. As the most hated fans in Britain, we would have identified with the personal besiegement of any United player in that position anyway. But because it was Eric, the personification of all the values we like to think of as United's - glamour, arrogance, sexiness, individualism - it became more than just a defence of a colleague or a mere desire not to lose one's best player. We were defending and supporting the very essence of the club.

If you went in search of the lost chord, the deepest resonance that the kick struck was with the older fans. Some have stood, then sat, and watched as something has drained away from United over recent years. One particular fanzine editor, quoted in the author's *As The Reds Go Marching On*, provided the best explanation of this special aspect of the Cantona–Red relationship.

It's all about respect. When we used to go to places like that in the '70s and '80s, the fact that we were United was a status to be respected, even feared. These suburban nobodies had to watch themselves: they knew they couldn't just say or do what they liked because if we got the hump over it, they got the kicking. And generally, we got respect and admiration when we deserved it, whether it be for the style with which we tried to play or for the devotion and power of our support. Now what do we get? We go to upstart shit-holes where they used to dream about the privilege of receiving United and what happens? They show no respect, they take the piss, they assault our players, they attack our coaches and sing 'Munich' at us. Who the f*ck do they think they are? Because they're in the safe, mollycoddled world of nineties football, they think they can get away with it. Ten years ago, if they'd behaved like that, we'd have beaten them to shit and pulled their crappy ground to pieces. At Selhurst Park, they thought they could come down to the touchline and call our players 'motherf*ckers' from the safety of a family stand. Ten years back, they wouldn't have dared; that stand would've been full of handy Reds who'd have stopped him opening his gob or getting anywhere near Eric. What Eric did was strike a blow for, not against, our self-respect. He just did what many of us would've done if we'd been near Simmonds. Simmonds didn't show Eric the respect he deserves; he thought he could act with impunity and he was wrong. You see, in that moment, Eric stood for Manchester United, and Simmonds for the rest of the Red-hating world. We might say we can't condone it but of course we can. It was a great last punch too.

And the final vindication for the fans? That Eric, when

he re-signed for us, should cite above all as the reason to stay at Old Trafford his desire not to disappoint the fans who'd supported him throughout. Every one of the thousands who sang for him, argued for him, signed for him or even fought for him can take a piece of the credit: Power to the People, Red-style.

City

I realize this is hard to believe but Manchester City once came very close to inflicting serious damage on Cantona's career. 6 March 1992: City 4, Leeds 0 and an anonymous Eric is told after the game that he would henceforth be used as a would-be 'supersub'. What a typical Wilko masterstroke to scapegoat his one true star; Eric bit the bullet this time but that afternoon set the two on the road to divorce, a split made inevitable by yet another 4–0 reverse at Maine Road in the autumn. Eric's every success with the Red Army has been one more dagger-blow of vengeance against his old sergeant, and he's profited in every game since against City to exact retribution for his humiliation that day. One of the requirements for any player seeking admission to the OT Pantheon of Heroes is to perform epic feats against any one of the mortal enemies – Leeds, Liverpool or City. A derby-winning goal is worth ten against Wimbledon; a leg-breaking tackle on a Dirty equals twenty fifty-fifties won at Palace. Why are the names Whiteside, Hughes and Robson so deeply engraved on the hearts of '80s Reds? Because they wielded the sword when it truly mattered. Eric appears to have chosen City as special recipients of his most sublime rapier blows; as any pissed-up Bitterman will admit, he looms large in every bed-wetting Blue nightmare.

A symbolic beginning: how fitting his debut was a derby. In the seven previous League meetings, we'd only won once, but in the Cantona era City have been barely able to live on the same pitch; Eric has come to symbolize the glamorous invincibility of United that eats away at the Blue soul. A harbinger of triumphs to come: Maine Road, 20 March 1993. United are in mid-wobble and a goal down, the final twenty approaching. A panther's pace, a salmon's leap and a King's header to save the day; he strikes the Denis Law salute and we're ready to crown him successor. Step two. No longer just content to extract Red bollocks from the fire, merely to save face – the alchemist must turn defeat into completed victory. There were few lower Red moments than half-time on 7 November 1993, stuck in the enclosure next to the Turkish Delighted Kippax, trying to block out the pre-dictable gleeful taunts. Yet Eric, the man who is supposed to go hiding under the stagecoach when the Injuns are circling, instead emerged to seize control. Dropping deep, crafting our fightback strategy, refusing to panic as the old United might've done – then suddenly appearing upfront in flashes of vision to smack home a double. Keano, the epitome of the last-ditch fighter, may have scored the winner but there was no doubt as to whose wizardry had spun this spectacular fairy-tale web around Grimm City. 'Two-nil up and f*cked it up': sweet soul music, boys.

After that watershed meeting, both Eric and we have

simply upped the amount of soured Bitter-urine we extract. On yet another of Eric's comebacks – as with the best stage-performers, these frequent absences only make Red hearts grow fonder – he imperiously dispatched a first-half pair the following April to place us back on the Double rails, one goal being such an accomplished *trompe l'oeil* that not even cameras could explain it. And when we rescheduled Bonfire Night for 10 November 1994 to reduce the last vestiges of Blue self-respect to ashes, no Ukrainian greed for goals could deflect the slavering tributes paid to Eric's masterly dominance. Truly, he took the piss with pride. Whatever is to come, and however many hilariously dodgy Cup penalties he might score, his place alongside the classic Derby Warriors is assured for all time. (>> Matt Busby)

Crisis

'Cantona' and 'crisis': they go together so naturally, like 'Quinn' and 'donkey', or 'Liverpudlian' and 'burglar'. Clearly, if you buy a passionate, wilful, free-spirited iconoclast, you can hardly expect to enjoy a lifetime of easy-going, Mabbuttish dependability. At least we were prepared from the start. We all knew Eric would be to Old Trafford as Elsie Tanner was to Coronation Street, a never-ending source of adventure, scandal, uproar and excitement – not to mention an enduring magnet for every flash suitor in the neighbourhood. (For Len Fairclough read Signor Moratti.) Normally, you learn not to fall in love with such tempestuous creatures, but with Eric it has proved impossible to resist.

The number of on-pitch Eric crises we've had to endure would in itself justify the establishment of a fans' trauma-counselling hotline (knowing United, an 0891 number with a ten-minute introduction). And examined objectively, his major suspensions have been all but devastating. The four-game Euro ban in '94/5 that covered the Barca fixtures cost us both our place in the last eight and our international self-respect. The 'Ides Of March' suspension in '93/4 depressed our League Cup Final performance and, had it been one game longer, could well have cost us the Double. As for the half-season exile in '94/5, would any dare contradict the hypothesis that we'd have walked the Double Double with Eric on board? Yet at each turn, few Reds could bring themselves to blame Eric. The soppy sentiment of a smitten husband who won't accept his wife's a tramp? So some bewildered pressmen suggested. But we couldn't ignore the fact that each crisis had been provoked by others who had gone virtually unpunished – Rothlisberger in Turkey, Callow at Highbury and Simmonds at Selhurst. (Sure, Rothlisberger may well have been removed later from several refs' lists, but that wasn't much use to us when getting panned at an Eric-less Nou Camp.) In any event, without Eric we wouldn't have been in any position to risk losing anything in the first place. Only the most churlish of small minds could have rounded on Eric at our time of common crisis.

Post-Selhurst, Red panic attacks are now not only induced by the sight of Eric going in for one of his 'tackles'. You can turn any Red face white merely by mentioning that Inter Milan (>>) have been in for him again. Twice during 1995 United fans across the world lived exactly the same death-row existence, waiting in dread to hear confirmation that Eric The Red was no more. They were horrendous days; however often we had all said in the past, Fergie included, that Eric's presence could never be taken for granted, the impending doom was unbearable, however predictable. The press, typically, were at their very worst in printing speculation rather than fact. In the three days before he re-signed in April, both 'experts' David Meek and Harry Harris pronounced him sold; during the late summer flap, only Richard Williams worked out the truth. The revelation that Eric's August wobbler had been provoked merely by an FA press comment about his practice matches, heard in the soul-sapping loneliness of a Novotel room, just goes to highlight how precarious this relationship can be. There will doubtless be further panics and crises to come; funnily enough, this reality only serves to make you appreciate his continuing presence more. He is like any loved one who's been through a few near-death experiences – you make the most of each new day as if it could be the last. We're all in too deep now to hold anything back anyway.

'D' is for . . .

Dave S

Editor of the anti-fascist standard-bearer Red Attitude. *One of the first to throw himself into the battle for the Cantona Defence Campaign, he immediately invented the 'political' mitigation soon taken up by the rest of us. Despite being on more hit-lists than EC himself, Dave and his crew remain as up for it as ever.*

If we are to understand the reason why United supporters took Monsieur Cantona to our hearts in the way we did, it's probably necessary to look at other developments at the club during his reign. United were undergoing their most successful period for decades, yet the club's hard-core support was being increasingly alienated by the relentless pursuit of profit. This was our world turned upside-down by corporate greed gone mad. The only thing we had left to believe in was Eric. We gasped in admiration at his audacious flicks and feints, we marvelled as moments of Cantonesque brilliance unlocked packed defences like a burglar armed with a fistful of skeleton keys, and we forgot for a while about extortionate ticket prices, all-seater stadiums, plcs and megastores. This was Eric the footballer, but Eric the man was also someone who had obviously thought a lot about the way the world works and furthermore had arrived at the right conclusions. He railed against injustice and intolerance in his frequent clashes with authority and he still defies the 'shitbags' who would see him banned for ever. No wonder we loved him.

The scale of United's nose-dive into crass commercial tackiness during the 1990s merely served to emphasize Eric's class, style and downright cool. Moreover, his dive into the crowd at Crystal Palace to attack Matthew Simmonds, a mouthy racist thug, added street-cred to his credentials. From footballer to anti-fascist street-fighter in one swoop! This was the antithesis of what United's commercial department were trying to achieve with their glossy magazines and Ryan Giggs duvet covers. It finally cemented the bond between the hard-core Red and Eric in a way that even the most majestic on-field performances never could. It wasn't necessary for the *Daily Mirror* to tell us that Simmonds was not only a loud-mouthed thug, but also a fascist sympathizer. Somehow we already knew, and somehow, maybe even subconsciously, I believe that Eric knew as well. Maybe it was the fact that Simmonds was wearing a leather jacket with a shirt and tie, the ultimate fashion *faux pas*, although as it happens *de rigueur* in fascist circles. Maybe it was Simmonds's boorish behaviour, which was an affront not only to Eric's family and upbringing but to his entire philosophy of life. Although not knowing Simmonds personally, Eric would have certainly known his type. His grandfather fled from Franco's fascist army in Spain and eventually settled in Marseilles, which was later to become a Front Nationale stronghold. If it was this that sent Eric homing in on his target with the unerring accuracy of an Exocet missile, then who could deny that this was the ultimate Cantona moment?

Diego Maradona

To the Little-Englander anti-Eric brigades, Cantona's frequent and passionate paeans of praise for the 'Argy basketball merchant' must seem proof positive that Eric is indeed in league with the Devil. You can see all the analogies ready to be made: filthy-tempered cheating dagoes, violent head-cases, arrogant preening prima donnas and so on. Indeed, the only footballer to be vilified within these shores as much as Eric in '95 was Maradona in '86 after the 'Hand of God' incident that aroused precisely the same ritualistic, xenophobic hysteria as Cantona's kung-fu. (Be honest – the greater injustice that day would've been an England victory. No team containing Terry Fenwick deserves to get anywhere near a World Cup semi.)

That Eric has such admiration for Maradona's football, placing him within a holy triumvirate alongside Pele and Platini, should go without saying. But in this age of the anti-hero, and of anti-heroism, Eric rightly points out that Maradona's gifts to football are too often forgotten amid the welter of scandal, insult and disapproval. In his book, Eric speaks of Maradona's 'feel of immortality . . . the mention of his name is enough to recall his performances'. Sadly, for many who allow themselves to be blinded by the gaudy glare of the detritus that litters Maradona's troubled life, those are not the images conjured up; perhaps Eric can see the danger that his own legacy to our memories will be similarly tainted. These days, discussion of Maradona is dominated by his supposed crimes, not by his achievements. But if he has to be discussed in such terms, Eric will take that debate on, for it raises issues central to his own experience. So he's taken recreational drugs, allegedly by the barrel-load – so what? As Eric – ever one to jump to the defence of a man's right to privacy – points out, Maradona was no Ben Johnson; snorting coke on a Wednesday night out in Naples has no relevance to his performance on a Sunday afternoon. As for the violent outbursts on the field, much less frequent than the myth has it, how often were they the result of provocation, of officials' indolence or of simple over-passionate commitment to his team? Eric, obviously, has understood that through harsh experience. There's no record of his views on Maradona shooting an air rifle at door-stepping journalists but even the soberest conjecture can imagine a certain amount of empathy, not to mention a hearty Gallic chuckle or two. (Let's face it: if you had Sadler, Harris and Co. at your gate, taking a pot-shot would be hard to resist.)

But it is Maradona's increasingly political role that has now drawn Eric's support, much to the hooting amusement of the press. Joining together to form an embryonic world players' union, the two of them have finally found a way to channel a mutual disgust, namely that corruption, money and power-crazed administrators are threatening to wreck what is left of football's purity. Both have suffered at the hands of capricious authority, both have been targeted for daring to slate the blazered buffoons and crooks who run their game. Eric has talked of the sullen realization that players are mere pawns, controlled by corrupt hypocrites who exercise power without true legitimacy. Cantona puts it simply: 'a system which pushes administrators to the forefront rather than players is in danger'. If Eric and Diego's final mission is to give the game to the players – and however mercenary some may be, they have a legitimate right to their own game which presidents and chairmen can never attain – then surely they deserve support not ridicule.

'E' is for . . .

Elba

The island of Elba: since Napoleon's little holiday there in 1814; the symbol of temporary, penultimate exile. And like the Emperor who shared a home island with Eric's own ancestors, Cantona has used his all too frequent Elban experiences to reassess, rebuild and return roaring to the acclaim of his legions. His critics may still predict a final voyage to St Helena for him but so far, as a Bonaparte contemporary said, I see no ships.

His French career was studded with banishments, lay-offs, suspensions and occasional self-denying ordinances. His subsequent marathon punishment in England may have been the most gruelling but at least he had had some sort of mental preparation. At each step he seems to have learned a particular lesson that has shaped his future conduct and strengthened his general resolve. Take perhaps the most difficult experience, his months off after injury at Marseilles. Close Cantona-watchers reckon that he has played slightly differently since that wrecking tackle-from-behind. He takes the ball with back wholly to goal far less often, preferring to manoeuvre side-on or facing: it means his ball control has to be even better, but he has succeeded. His lengthy banishment from Tapie's Marseille taught him that the last thing you can sacrifice is self-respect; he had been right to refuse to kow-tow. By accepting his exile without pleading for mercy he had been rewarded with a first honour at Montpellier and the gratifying sight of Olympique Marseilles coming back for him caps in hand. Similarly, by brazening out his international ban after the 'shitbag' farrago, he actually returned in a stronger position (Michel's sacking having been a vindication of sorts) and eventually became captain. Doubtless his English holiday courtesy of Graham Kelly Travel has had its effect too. (>> Quietism)

But surely the greatest existential crisis in exile he has undergone was during the weeks of inaction following his 'retirement' from football at Nimes. This was no Bowie-at-Hammersmith sleight of hand: he was utterly determined to hang up his boots for good. He sought tranquillity above all, and that meant leaving France and never entering the maelstrom of a football stadium again. And for the best part of a fortnight he revelled in the relief: 'I had never felt so much at ease with myself.' Refusing to answer the phone lest he be dissuaded, and supported by Isabelle despite the threat to their material well-being, he lost himself in rural pursuits and contemplation. To any observer, it appeared that he was St Helena-bound. And yet . . .

Eric knows only too well the existentialist doctrine that says you are defined by how you act not by who you are. He had long since chosen to be an artist and to use football as the vehicle; his success in that allowed him to be defined as he had dreamed. But if your life consists of bumming about on beaches, knocking up the odd abstract and slobbering about in domesticity, it doesn't matter how much you still claim to be an artist within when the existential reality is contradictory. Eric now admits that he knew something was missing but didn't want to admit it – he missed the action, the physicality and artistry of football. The more the days passed, the more he knew he wasn't being true to himself, which he had himself decreed was the greatest moral failing. Still he refused to concede defeat to himself, until Michel Platini found the magic formula. By offering him help to find a new challenge abroad, he made Eric realize that it wasn't retirement he sought but an alternative that brought the same kind of complete, radical, Ground Zero departure. And you can't get much further from France's cultured and genteel environment than the neolithic primitivism of Leeds, can you? (>> Yorkshire)

Existential Eric

During the Morlino–Cantona interview in *United We Stood*, Eric makes the most open and important declaration about his philosophy: 'Deep down I am an existentialist. At first I learned existentialism from Camus and Sartre but then I found my own particular route.' As you can appreciate, it's the explanation of the second half of that statement that is our ultimate destination, but that will not make any sense unless we grasp what Eric first extracted from the works of these Left Bank gurus.

Camus was the better writer, the more appealing bloke, certainly the greater footballer and, in retrospect, the one who made the right choice in the seismic late 1940s Camus–Sartre political split. But Sartre was the existentialist theorist of choice for the Parisian black polo-neck brigade and it is his development of Kierkegaard, Heidegger and Husserl that is most relevant here.

Sartre's is above all a philosophy of freedom, based on the first principle that 'existence precedes essence'. There is no such thing as a given human nature which dictates what we do; man first of all exists as a free agent and defines himself by his actions. We are what we make of ourselves; in fact, we are condemned to be free since there is no natural law or objective morality. Man must choose to construct the meaning of his own world, create his own morals and values and take full responsibility for his actions. Society may then do its worst to you but the individual is really only answerable to himself; there is no responsibility greater than the responsibility to be authentic and true to yourself. Naturally, there is no God; life's only purpose is that you must use your freedom and make a commitment – the French buzz-word being *engagement* –to political or artistic activism. Refusal to do so is an indication of *mauvaise foi* – literally 'bad faith' – which is the worst insult you can throw at an exis.

If you can't see any of this in the actions and words of Cantona, then you haven't been paying attention. Existentialism is the ultimate expression of Kantian autonomy and, in Scruton's phrase, 'an imaginative dramatization of the post-romantic soul'; it is an almost irresistible port of call for any free-spirited voyager whose central concern is individualism, liberty and the usages of freedom. It would be astonishing then if Cantona were *not* an existentialist. Indeed, it is no fancy to suggest that if Sartre were alive today, he would be a confirmed Cantonista. He has written that the true saint-figure for the modern intellectual is not the hero but the anti-hero who goes through life revealing the moral emptiness of bourgeois conformity, a figure such as Jean Genet who demonstrates that all morals are subjective and that freedom is the right to disobey any law your own morality rejects. Cantona admires Genet hugely; weren't his kung-fu kicks, shirt-throwing and Riolaci-baiting precisely the sort of *épater les bourgeois* outrages in which Genet used to specialize? There's a paradoxical trap here, however, which Eric has revealingly avoided falling into: although one might call oneself an existentialist in general terms, to go as far for example as saying 'I am a disciple of Sartre' is in itself a classic exhibition of *mauvaise foi* and proof that you've entirely missed the point, copping someone else's entire individual belief system which in itself is telling you to go and find your own! (Remember the balcony scene in *Life Of Brian*?) Eric has indeed shaped his own variant of existentialism and one in which essentialism still plays a part, a modern compromise for a modern thinker. (>> Family Values)

Exotica

*T*he *ground-breaking record label, whose 'Bend It' series delighted kitsch connoisseurs world-wide, hit the charts in '95 with the 'Eric The King' single and the epic* Cantona Album. *Now intensely trendy as the Easy boom takes hold, Jim Phelan, the noted athlete, aesthete of cheese and dreamer who runs the label, ruminates on heroic identification.*

When I was a kid, every Saturday morning I used to go to the Edgeley Cinema just down the road from Edgeley Park. On the way back up Castle Street and all along Shaw Heath, I'd be the baddy from a Hopalong Cassidy film and shoot up every shop I passed. Later it was the Black Knight of Faldor, and when I got into comics I metamorphosized into Alf Tupper, the Tough of the Track (an adopted characterization that has yet to leave me).

In my teens I was a mean and moody James Dean (complete with quiff), for a couple of years more comfortable as Brian Jones, but when Georgie came on the scene, there was no contest. Although I rode an ancient Lambretta whilst he drove his harem of Miss Worlds about in a Lotus, and our footballing talents were a universe apart, our personas were intrinsically linked via Old Trafford and totally interchangeable for the whole time he played for United.

For novelty's sake, I spent a few years being me. At odd times I'd identify with Coe and Ovett setting new world records but apart from that, nothing, not a twinge of envy or cupidity for film, pop or sports star until now . . . now, in the middle of my allotted span, I have become Eric Cantona. And now I'm mean, moody and totally magnificent; I read poetry, paint abstract pictures and speak in philosophical parables of trawlers, sardines and seagulls. I treat the press with the aloof disdain they deserve. I strut the catwalk with my magnificent physique and handsome Latin looks. I have the sexiest of accents and as a proud Frenchman I do not suffer fools or racists on or off the pitch. I defy all conventions and I play football like a god.

As for alternatives . . . what about Beardsley? Despite his obvious talent and admirable longevity, who on earth would identify with a wasp-chewing dwarf bearing the legends 'world's worst haircut' and 'United reject'? Or Rush – prolific scorer he may be but that proboscis and the inability to string together enough incomprehensible scouse grunts to form even the most rudimentary of sentences makes him an instant non-starter. Or Gazza: the man could cry for England but compared to Eric he is merely a bloated Geordie buffoon who could only attract a fan-following as dodgy as his haircuts and knees. So there's no choice. It's got to be Eric on all counts. The new renaissance man is amongst us and what's more he plays for United. But what of Eric; when he fantasizes, who could he become . . .?

'F' is for . . .

Family Values

Jean-Paul Sartre (<< Existential Eric), in his efforts to prioritize existence over essence, never denied that man had to face up to the realities of his situation within the world. By the time we've reached the age where we are looking to define and exert our freedom to act, we are all marked by inescapable influences. One is born into a class, a gender, a language group and a nation; add to that one's genetic inheritance and the fact, as we now know, that one's IQ is also hugely shaped by the first three years of life experience, and the result would appear to be much of the essence of a human's nature. Sartre turned this 'problem' around to his advantage: it was precisely how you responded to these situations and constraints that constituted and defined your freedom. You decide what is to be made of them and, by impli-cation, how little you will allow these elements of your supposed 'essence' to interfere with your existential free-dom of action to create your true essence.

The key here is to recall that existentialism's high point was the 1940s and early 1950s. The literature was aimed at a generation that sought to reinvent itself, to wipe the slate clean. In the era of defeat, Vichy and post-war trauma, the adherents of Sartre and Camus were only too keen to discard their upbringings, to rid themselves of the rotten lessons taught by their parents, to give new free actions the power to eradicate whatever they did wrong after 1939. It was a philosophy of complete liberation; it allowed you to be defined by how you acted today, not by some entrapping notion that you remained fundamentally bourgeois, defeatist, collaborationist or decadent because that was what your family were like. Modern France had found a way to redefine the adjective 'French'. And for a time that also meant traditional family values were out; individualistic reinvention was in.

But Eric grew up in an entirely different world to that of 1946 Paris. What if you not only recognize the power of those elements that make up your 'essence' but actively welcome them? What if the values taught by your family are entirely consistent with those you would choose for yourself? What if you are not ashamed to speak of your own 'human nature' and instead wish to work with it rather than against it? It's entirely understandable that Sartre, with his ridiculously prissy *haute bourgeois* upbringing, his parents' generation's failures and his own rather nasty demeanour as a kid, should wish to cut himself off from all that and reinvent himself as a pro-prole Marxist warrior. But Cantona, having examined himself, his nature and his family values in some depth as a young man, has discovered no such desire. He got dealt a good hand and was allowed to play it by parents who shared his Rousseauesque notions.

So if, as an independent adult exercising his new-found freedom, he chooses to take an existentialist view of life generally, he hasn't felt it necessary to throw out all notions of essentialism in return. Therefore he can speak in the same breath of his admiration for Sartreanism and total individual freedom yet also of his belief in being true to his family's values, his own essential nature and of listening to the Inner Child. Academic philosophers will jump all over such a synthesis but life is too short to discuss phenomenological absurdities and why red is red. You take what works where you can find it and if it helps you make sense of your existence, who's complaining? (>> 'Lodger')

Fearlessness

Strong, hard and fearless – that's how Old Trafford likes 'em. Who were the greatest Red heroes of the 1980s? Hughes, Whiteside and Robson, warriors all three. Put 1980s United in a Continental setting and maybe contemporaries such as Jesper Olsen, Arnold Muhren and Ray Wilkins would have thrived more; perhaps they had the greater technique and skill, although Norm at his best could argue the point. But we play in England, not some slow-fast-slow fancy-dan foxtrot Euroleague, and only the toughest need apply. And one point upon which all his contemporaries agreed when his move to England was first mooted was, as Eric remarked, that 'my heart and legs were made for British football'.

So the English hatchetmen who were doubtless awaiting just another effete Continental with lipsmacking anticipation have been richly disappointed. Six foot of pure muscle, power and strength has been more than a match for the clogging attentions of the Jones brigade. There is no corner of an English pitch Eric fears to tread. Allied to his physical hardness is his mental strength; as Houllier remarks, 'he's solid, mentally very very strong and is never afraid'. The odd mishap aside, his perform-ances under pressure have been exemplary. On each of his many comebacks, the spotlight glare burning brighter every time, he has been the acme of cool, concentrated focus; every crucial penalty is dispatched with the unerr-ing nerve and precision of a surgeon. If you have cour-age, anything is possible: a man who can take on seven assailants simultaneously as Eric once did is clearly not lacking in that department.

So his fearlessness comes from both mental and physi-cal strength. He is self-evidently your archetypal hard bastard, with the strutting body language, killer's gaze and menacing hirsute duskiness to match – the proverbial unwelcome, dark-alley encounter. But his greatest trials have been spiritual: exile, awaiting sentencing and pro-fessional failures. And that is why his mental strength is the more impressive. Speaking from experience, I know of few more testing moments than that which holds your very liberty in the balance. If you can retain a manly serenity in that, then you can think yourself strong. Eric's supremely cool behaviour at that very moment spoke of a man who has strength because he has been within himself and knows what he can take. Introspection is often seen as indulgence but in fact it's the *sine qua non* of a meaningful existence. He knows exactly who he is and how strong that person can be. And as he has nothing to fear from within himself, there is little without which can frighten him either.

Fergie

. . . or perhaps that should be 'Fergie and Kiddo'; as with another legendary duo, Butch and Sundance, the quiet side-kick never gets enough credit. Not an omission made by Eric, naturally: in his book he spends as many words praising Brian as he does Alex. It is easily forgotten, in the understandable rush to worship at the Ferguson feet, that most of a United player's working life is spent training with Kidd and that consequently his influence is daily, relentless and telling. Eric was always one to treat training with an unusual reverence: 'this is where I learn to be a better artist' is a somewhat different attitude to the English pro's three-laps-and-off-for-a-pint mentality. In Kidd, he's found a fellow believer. No player leaves United without remarking upon the originality, brilliance and entertainment offered by a Kidd session. Backed by his frequent research expeditions to superior schools – meaning Amsterdam and Milan, not Lillishall – Kidd's own has become a technical masterclass featuring Eric as star pupil-cum-instructor. Never forget too the kudos Kidd brings from his playing days. Most players cannot help but find extra credibility in a would-be teacher who has actually done the business himself, and Eric in particular has always reserved his greatest approbation for the Tiganas and Platinis who have

already practised what they preach to him. Some Rob-
sonites fear Old Trafford will crumble if Kidd eventually
becomes manager; none would dare suggest Eric shares
that opinion.

Alex Ferguson is often accused by outsiders of being
blinded by his love for Eric. Not only will he never
criticize him in public but he appears to treat him differently from the rest, breaching that English collectivist
doctrine that you don't play favourites within a team.
Not only is all that probably true but surely any loyal
Red would thank God that it is so. When it comes to
dealing with Eric, Fergie has two priceless assets. Firstly,
their temperamental similarities which were once predicted to cause a mutual explosion but have instead
bound them together in mutual understanding. Fergie
was a hard, hot-headed, passionate striker, prone to outbursts but 'only for the right reasons' – not only can he
see his own traits in Eric but he sees in him the player
he dreamed of being. For a manager with such a pat-
ernalistic instinct towards his players, what else could he
see in Eric but a spiritual son? He goes as far as to say
that Eric is one of only three players he's never lost his
temper with; so much for the doom merchants' predictions. Secondly, Fergie's greatest man-management skill
is his ability to treat every player as an individual without
ruining the collective spirit. If that means he can ignore
something Eric does which from any other player would
bring forth flying tea cups a-plenty, so be it. He can offer
Eric the personal, tailored attention he always sought
and with it a separate moral code between player and
manager. It is justified because it benefits both the indi-

viduals and the collective as a whole; perhaps this is that
Scottish twist on Protestantism that has made Ferguson
unique amongst managers.

There has only been one slippage, when Fergie's first
post-Selhurst reaction was to admit defeat and invite
offers, but that was redeemed when he chased Eric to
Paris later in the year to bring home the prodigal son.
It could be said that they saved each other's careers at
that crossroads in 1992 but they are surely bound
together by more than that. It is their mutual belief in
the art of football that matters. The best illustration of
that shared credo, and of why Ferguson succeeded where
Wilkinson failed, emerges from Leeds's defeat in
Stuttgart. Eric had taken a knock but battled on trying
to save the game. One-nil down, he saw a potentially
devastating cross-field pass which just failed; Stuttgart
scored from the interception. Wilkinson bellowed
'f*cking hell' and took him off, a decisive moment in
their impending divorce. Compare this Ferguson quote:
'When finely tuned players like Cantona attempt something difficult in the last third and it goes wrong, no
problem. That's not carelessness but a footballer taking
risks with his craft. I admire and applaud that kind of
nerve and audacity – in my camp, that is never going to
be criticized.' Written in almost Cantonesque language,
that view expresses so much; it is the difference between
Wilkinson and Ferguson, between United and the rest,
between functionalism and art. As a philosophy, it unites
Govan and Caillols more than ancient Jacobinism ever
could.

'G' is for . . .

Garageflower

*O*ne *of the many pseudonyms and* noms de plume *used by the only Burnage Boy whose infamy rivals the Gallaghers – the singing streaker Peter Boyle. Founder of the shadowy Eric The King Appreciation Society, leader of pop group The K-Standers, roving Defender of the Faith throughout Eric's trials in 1995 and one-man terrace song factory, here he recalls a close encounter with royalty.*

As I left home for another predictable night rehearsing *Songs from the Bathtub* at the Peveril, I had no idea how memorable the night would turn out to be. At around nine p.m., we were interrupted by the landlady and told there was someone downstairs we would probably be interested to see. We casually strolled down the stairs into the pub; it was at this point that my knees went weak, very weak. I stared in disbelief across the main bar into the vault and there, playing bar football, was none other than Monsieur Genius himself. Now although I'd had the pleasure of meeting him once before, outside the players' hotel in Hungary with about a dozen other

Reds, this was my local on a wet Thursday night and it felt different, unreal.

I entered the vault and assumed a place at the bar a few feet from Eric and his friends. On noticing my United hat, Eric politely acknowledged my presence. 'Remember Hungary,' I spluttered, 'outside the hotel?' He smiled and nodded. One of his friends approached me, having heard that I'd written a song about the King. 'Not one but two,' I replied, knees trembling with excitement.

Moments later, after I'd had a quick nerve-calming whisky, Eric came across to where I was now sitting. 'You have a song about me?' he asked. 'Yeah, yeah,' I replied, 'do you know Lily the Pink?' After a quick rendition of Eric The King, Eric asked me for a copy of one of the tapes we were recording; I was given his mate Claude's address where the great man could receive it direct.

A little later as they left, I shook hands with him and explained I was honoured, to which he responded with a shrug of the shoulders as if to say, 'Don't be daft'. I left the boozer on cloud nine and had to pinch myself for half an hour to convince myself that it had really happened: 'I waited years for this, I never thought this night would ever be, this close to me . . .'

Goals

'**A** good goal is one that is both important and beautiful', Eric the aphorist once famously quipped. Not something with which Saint Gary Diarrhoea would concur perhaps but a good maxim for Eric to use to set himself apart. Few men score such a proportion of beautiful rather than plain goals; similarly few score such a high proportion of crucial match-savers and winners. On the *Principia Cantona*, not too many of Lineker's would make the grade, four-yard tap-ins being less than gorgeous as a rule. Similarly, take out all those Shearer hat-tricks racked up against already beaten teams in nothing matches – doesn't leave so many does it?

Eric was originally bought for goals and hasn't failed us – an absolute rarity for a bought-in United striker – and here a delegation from the Eric The King Appreciation Society selects ten *bon buts* on the Cantona criteria for you to argue over, all beautiful and important.

1. v. CHELSEA, FA Cup Final 14.5.94

We had to choose one spot-kick to represent all those flawless exhibitions of sang-froid and technique that contain their own special beauty. The second at Wembley gets the nod: it effectively won the game and the Double and had the utter cheek to be placed in exactly the same spot as the first.

2. v. MANCHESTER CITY 23.4.94

On his post-Ides of March comeback, his double changed the face of our League season. The sleight of foot that slipped the ball under a bamboozled Coton for his second on half-time was the purest instinct springing from innate class, and it killed any remaining Blue challenge stone dead.

3. v. WIMBLEDON 20.2.94

Key moment on road to Wembley victory. A stunning touch and dip volley from outside the box cracked open the match and led to a second-half procession. Possibly the most replayed moment of Eric's spontaneous magic.

4. v. BLACKBURN 22.1.95

Deceptively brilliant header that found the only few square inches available to him in Flowers's net and required awesome control to get into position. His last positive act of the year threw us a last title life-line and gave us the important moral victory of a double over the so-called champions.

5. v. MANCHESTER CITY 10.11.94

Tremendous crashing finish set up by his own unbeliev-able ankle-flick taken at full pelt; opened up the game, put Blue heads down and inspired goal-fest rout.

6. v. SHEFFIELD UTD 9.1.95

Drop-dead gorgeous drop-shot that seemed to stun even Eric himself; just as Sheffield threatened to do us, he set us up for another Wembley run.

7. v. ARSENAL 19.9.93

Arguably the most remarkable indirect free-kick since Willie Carr's. Conjured up those TV images of Gulf War missiles; seemed to finish Arsenal as a force in '93.

8. v. MANCHESTER CITY 7.11.93
Started and finished a supremely sweet move for the match-turning equalizer; pure technique and intelligence throughout. With twelve to go, it made the most thrilling derby win almost inevitable and restored post-Turkey morale.

9. v. QPR 30.10.93
Untypical solo Eric: a dazzling, overpowering run from halfway capped by a venomous, deadly accurate bottom-corner drive from twenty-plus yards. The goal brought us level and cracked them open to defeat.

10. v. MANCHESTER CITY 20.3.93
The swoop of an eagle to bury brilliantly for a copybook header. Pace, timing and position all perfect with top Law pose to follow. Saved our derby skins and kept title challenge on course.

Le Grand Geste

One of the first things you teach kids about the history of French foreign policy is the concept of *la gloire*: not only did French leaders have to succeed but they had to do so gloriously – the public demanded it. The British method of patient alliance-building and careful incremental gains was anathema; the French loved the dramatic sweep, the bold adventure, *le grand geste*. The result could be either the fabulous, barnstorming victory at Austerlitz or 100,000 beaten troops freezing their balls off in Moscow. Napoleon tried too many heel-flicks and cross-field passes for his own good but he remains the greatest French hero ever. And consciously or not, Eric has absorbed the historical lesson.

Many current Cantona observers share Mrs Thatcher's legendary distaste for this Gallic flavouring. She used to complain that whilst the Brits examined the nuts and bolts of the EC's operation, the French would swan off to build grandiose dreams of a united Europe. Eric has similarly often stood accused of seeking *le grand geste* at the expense of both himself and his team. Wasn't the infamous Stuttgart Interception (>> Fergie) which hastened his departure from Leeds a prime example? Even Platini once opined that Eric only wanted to score a goal if it was a beautiful one and that he too often looked for the grand gesture. National coach Jacquet weighed in too: 'Sometimes he lacks the killer instinct . . . he is in love with the ball, seeking a gesture for its own sake.' After all, didn't Eric himself provide further ammunition with his quip about a good goal being one that is both important and beautiful?

Any United fan would surely argue that, as regards Eric in the box, these complaints are way past their sell-by date. He has mucked in with the tap-ins and scuff shots like a good 'un; accusations of headstrong wastefulness tended to be the domain of Giggs, Hughes and Keane, not Eric. But outside the box, well, perhaps there's something to it. Yet as Ferguson himself has noted, Cantona's ambition is welcomed not denigrated at Old Trafford because there's a fundamental difference between Cantona's cock-ups and those of other players. When Eric loses possession away from the tackle, what is the usual cause? Almost always it's the failure of a grand gesture, usually the outrageous flick that misfires or the forty-yard pass that falls off-target. He has failed in trying to attempt the glorious rather than the mundane, the balls that when successful create more for United than ten simple five-yarders. On any profit and loss account of Eric's more ambitious plays, he is overwhelmingly in credit and has the medals to prove it. Listen to the crowd reaction when, say, Sharpe buggers up an easy lay-off. They growl and curse: he's failed the simplest task and deserves the smack. Then witness the response when an Eric heel-flick just misses splitting the defence: they're either silent (as if no one will admit to having seen him make a mistake) or they emit a wistful 'oh Eric', more in regret than anger. It seems that Fergie and the fans are at one in this, alone in a league dominated by the Wilkinson mentality: Old Trafford was built on the ambition that underpins *le grand geste*. Even David Batty knows how to play it safe and simple. When you're trying to create football for the heavens, sometimes you have to aim for the stars.

The *Guardian*

The supernova that followed the Eric-star explosion at Selhurst Park was, for the most part, of a predictable hue. The tabloid guttersnipes joined the more pompous denizens of the 'qualities' and appearance-fee-hungry ex-pros to construct a gallows; the United fanzines and loyal Reds in general threw their subjective passions into trying to cut down the noose. Both played a part in opening the way for a third, most welcome contribution – the ranks of the uncommitted coming forward to defend the accused. Disgusted by the sanctimonious excess of Eric's persecutors and attracted by the first, lone arguments of Crerand & Co., such contributions helped redefine the public mood within days; by the time Eric received his first court sentence, the voices of sympathy seemed to be drowning out the blood-lust howls of the mob. The following extracts are typical of the testimonials that began to appear in independent columns and letters pages all over the shop.

Commentators carp on about 'professionalism' and 'showing an example' and disregard totally the human element, as if no soccer player is permitted emotion. Nonsense. The proper condemnation should be directed at those who have blown up a relatively trivial, over-emotional reaction into an incident on a par with the assassination of Archduke Ferdinand. (*Evening Standard* letters)

Should Cantona be made the scapegoat for an incident initiated by a known racist and criminal convicted of attempted armed robbery? The FA must be careful their decision does not demean this season's competitions by ensuring a victory for racist and xenophobic abuse. (D. Wynne, Director of the Manchester Metropolitan University's Institute of Popular Culture)

Mr Cantona in prison, why? He did good work, kicked the shouty roast beef tomato in the balls. (Jésus and Paulo from Barça, *Loaded* letters)

So all wogs begin at Calais again. The sub-plot to the Cantona incident is clear, it dates back to Agincourt. Good on you, Eric, for confronting mindless, ignorant bigots in the most direct way. (G. Hetherton, *Observer* letters)

For 'assaulting' Terry Lloyd, he has been upbraided by the same sanctimonious Pecksniffs who criticized his first outburst. But the real villain is Mr Lloyd. He poked his nose into the life of a man trying to have a private holiday with his pregnant wife. Being a red-blooded Gaul, Eric rose to his woman's defence. If Lloyd had any dignity, he would've taken his punishment like a man. ('Man We Hate' column, *Mail* OS)

Cantona is simply a classic example of a passionate and caring male primate displaying protective behaviour towards the woman and unborn child he loves. If you see him in this context, even his sweeping Grand-Jetes demonstrate, like the first miraculous kick inside the womb, that there is a kind of symbiosis there between father and unborn child. Far from being reviled, he should be applauded. (*Guardian* column)

Eric's spectacular assault on some odious thug was an utter joy. It's what we all want, our creative geniuses touched by self-destructive madness, you know it is. Nothing is more inspirational than the artist whose expression is dictated by spirit rather than sense, nothing so alluring as a talent with a dark side. For what it's worth, and as befits his unarguable status as Britain's most rock 'n' roll footballer, Eric Cantona may consider the *Melody Maker* and all who sail in her firmly on his side in the trying months to come. Even the Chelsea fans. (Viewpoint column, *Melody Maker*)

In 1937, Dixie Dean was applauded by a policeman when he jumped into the crowd and punched a man who'd called him a 'black bastard'. Only the thug was surprised, as were the two Forest fans who felt the sting of Brian Clough's admonishing slap. Alberto Tarantini waded into his own supporters in 1978, an action which went largely unpublicized and unpunished. Graham Kelly's declaration that Cantona's indiscretion was "without precedent" obviously does not stand up under close scrutiny. (*Observer* column)

Suppose Mr Cantona had been an ordinary member of the public and just a few yards outside the ground had aimed a kick, which did little or no harm, at a man who had been abusing his race and mother. Would it have caused a ripple of concern? Of course not. Would the police, if called, have bothered to do anything? Very unlikely. The most that would have happened is that he'd have walked off with a police caution. As it is, he's been fined, banned and faces further idiocy from the FA and that ludicrously inept group, the Crown Prosecution Service. They should all be spending their time on real criminals. Leave Eric – and Paul Ince too – to get on with their lives. (M. Winner, *News of the World* column)

Manchester United should not sack Eric Cantona, say our readers, who voted NO by 82 per cent in last night's poll, which brought the biggest response since the Myra

Hindley poll. (*Manchester Evening News* front page – were even some Blues impressed by EC?)

When I read about the fan, it was obvious that he was a right-wing prat. I wish Cantona had gone for his face as well. (Martin Carr, a BooRadley and LFC fan)

To be honest, I loved the Cantona kicking. I was just marvelling over it. I just hate that kid he attacked. That's the beauty of football. Cantona is like a coiled spring and that's why everybody loves him. (3D, Massive Attack and a Bristol City fan)

I thought fair play to Cantona. I wish he'd knocked his head off. He should've killed him. It's a joke that because you're a sporting personality you're not allowed to have a human reaction to something. (Jarvis Cocker of Pulp and a SWFC fan)

I don't feel an ounce of pity for that bastard supporter. I bet his arsehole dropped on the floor when Eric came over. (Andy Townsend, Aston Villa)

You don't have to look very long and hard at Mr Matthew Simmonds of Thornton Heath to conclude that Eric Cantona's only mistake was to stop hitting him. The more we discovered about Mr Simmonds, the more Cantona's assault looked like the instinctive expression of a flawless moral judgement.

That last quote came from the handsome Cantona inamorato Richard Williams, the true heir to McIlvanney (dream on Paddy Barclay). At the time he was at the

Independent but soon transferred to the *Guardian*. Perhaps paper and writer saw in each other the love of originality and the gift of seeing beyond the obvious. It always amuses me to hear Reds who complain about the scumbag media and awful football reporting respond, when asked what paper they read, 'Oh, the *Mirror/ Sun*.' Is an extra twenty pence too much to receive the burnished wit and style of the majestic David Lacey and new signing Williams thus never needing to complain again? Fittingly, the *Guardian* took up its liberal cudgels and provided by far the best coverage of the trials of le Dieu, often dragging the rest of decent press opinion with it. Not only was Lacey the sole journo to spot that Simmonds appeared to have thrown something at Eric, other writers dug up precedents, exposed the absurdities of the police inquiry and generally corrected the rubbish being spouted in Murdoch's rags. Then in two cracking editorials, quoted from below (both apparently written by a Leeds United supporter), they drew up the case for the defence.

Aren't we all rushing to judgement? At least allow a wider case to be heard before the best player in Britain is banished. There's no hypocrite like an English hypocrite. Cantona will be sacrificed in the name of preserving the values of our game. The fact that the game is synonymous with greed, failure and violence will be ignored. So will consistency. Cantona was sent off for a foul far less serious . . . than Bosnich's on Klinsmann which went entirely unpunished. Indignation in football is notoriously selective. Retaliation is wrong but in context it can be understandable. In some circumstances it is morally and even legally condoned. Cantona was provoked. Can the same be said on behalf of the 'fan'? Was his abuse justifiable in any circumstances whatever? Cantona's action was wrong; but in a way it was also a truly moral outburst.

OOH AH: A JAIL SENTENCE TOO FAR. Cantona was sentenced to two weeks in prison because he is 'a high profile public figure looked up to by many young people'. Mrs Pearch missed a major opportunity to demonstrate the benefits of community penalties yesterday. None of the arguments for upholding this sentence is persuasive. Pearch has breached a fundamental principle of the Criminal Justice Act. Parliament has made it clear that prison must be reserved for offences 'so serious that only prison is justified'. Cantona's kick does not fall into that category.

When the rest of the mouth-foaming press sought the easy route to please the ABU majority, the *Guardian* stood firm. Remember that next time you're handing over money that pays the enormous salaries of the jackals at MGN and News International.

'H' is for . . .

'Heroes'

This is the age of the anti-hero; moreover, the very concept of 'heroism' is about as *outré* as one can get. In Britain, hero-status may last a week, about as long as it takes for a Sunday tabloid to get the weaponry together to smash both hero and pedestal for ever. Was it Johnny Rotten who called upon us to 'kill your idols'? (As he is now himself an idol of sorts, we await his impending demise.) What was once a healthy impulse, particularly in a country raddled by deference and Establishment censorship, has now become solely destructive. Currently, nothing is as uncool for a celeb as public meditation upon the heroes you worshipped; much better to spit upon the graves of your ancestors and proclaim your genius is entirely original. Should you make the mistake à la Noel Gallagher, of admitting your youthful infatuation, you must follow it immediately with some 'ballsy' disrespect, like claiming your first two albums have emulated The Beatles: in yer coke-induced dreams, Bluenose. Not so Eric: as with his existentialism, lack of irony and belief in traditional virtues, his readiness to exalt his heroes and speak of what they taught him is a refreshing throw-back to a bygone age. These, then, are Eric's top gurus, based on the number of times he's mentioned them in interviews. (>> Platini, Diego Maradona and Rimbaud, who get their own entries because he name-checks them every five minutes . . .)

Jim Morrison

The footballer-artist approaches every game as Jim took his gigs; one must endeavour to make each a true *performance*, not merely an appearance, even if that risks failure. When reaching for the stars, you sometimes fall back into the gutter, in Morrison's case with your knob hanging out of your keks. Eric has singled out Morrison as being the purest expression of the liberated artist who brings a sense of freedom to the listener. If his art broke the bounds of what subject matter rock could tackle – incest, patricide, sodomy, acid voyages; hey, all the good stuff – then Morrison too lived a life beyond normal boundaries. Like Eric, Jim was seen as a danger to society, a dreadful role model, a man with his own unbreakable moral code; just don't be falling asleep in any bathtubs Eric.

Marlon Brando

Often bracketed by Eric alongside would-be Method actor, and all-round embarrassment, Mickey Rourke; let us dwell on the Dylan rather than the Donovan. Interestingly, Eric has spoken of his identification with Brando's 'inner fragility that is concealed by his outward strength' – a rare admission of vulnerability. As he was spotted carting Brando's Byzantine autobiography around this

year, we can assume that Eric has appreciated the Cantonesque episodes in Brando's life: the way he hijacked
his own Oscar presentation to highlight political injustice; the frequent bust-ups with studio moguls and
bread-head execs; the way he improvised, relying on
instinct and spontaneity, throughout the last reel of
Apocalypse Now. And the two most Cantonesque Brando
roles? Surely as the rebel in both *The Wild One* ('whatcha
rebelling against?' – 'whatcha got?') and *On The Waterfront*, a metaphor for Eric's stand against corrupt authority if ever there was one.

Johann Cruyff
That initial, contemporary footballing idol of childhood
is always special; for the eight-year-old Eric, Cruyff was
not only self-evidently the best on view but the most
stylish and elegant. However much he admired Beckenbauer, Cruyff was the one to love: Eric felt as robbed as
the rest of us who saw Holland lose in 1974. Thanks to
this infatuation, Eric became drawn to Dutch football as
a whole, the influence still apparent when he appeared
on *The Bootroom* last year; Cruyff as a manager and coach
remains as attractive to Eric as ever and the suspicion
must be that one day he will fulfil the ambition to play
for him. Damn.

Antoine de Saint-Exupéry
Author of *Le Petit Prince*, possibly the most loved book
in the French language. Ostensibly a children's book but
venerated by adults, it speaks to the Inner Child (>>)
and is thus unsurprisingly one of Eric's top Desert Island

choices. The guy was also a genuine, non-collaborating wartime hero as a pilot – bit of a rarity in France – which only adds to the tough but tender, Brando-ish combination that Eric digs.

Bruce Lee

Not quite as dodgy a selection as Mickey Rourke but clearly an obvious one in the light of recent history. Apparently Eric even had the kitsch classic Lee poster on his '70s bedroom wall (next to Farrah Fawcett?) and, like every other seven-year-old of the time, spent many playground hours pulling ridiculous kung-fu poses. You can offer a defence that Lee's oeuvre of low-budget martial arts flicks is being reassessed in France as containing deeper allegorical and spiritual insights; but then again, the French think Jerry Lewis is a genius. Not even the rock-legend-style early death can stop this name conjuring up only the strains of Carl Douglas's horrendous Number One.

Pierre Ambrogiani

Painter of the Marseilles school that Eric places on a par with the Impressionists, undoubtedly brilliant at capturing the colours and spirit of Provence. Introduced to Eric at an early age by his father, Ambrogiani exhibitions became as common a day out for young Eric as the Vélodrome. Down there, they've also got Camoin, Chabaud, Ferrari and Cézanne to admire: we get Damien Hirst. Ewe despair . . .

David Bowie

An obvious choice, perhaps, at least in his 1970s incarnation. A man prepared to risk being called pretentious by reaching for the higher things in life, a reinventer and eternal traveller from Station to Station, looking for the New Career in a New Town (>> 'Lodger'), a man who understands image projection and the value of maintaining the element of surprise. (As Eric says, 'Do the unexpected: it's never a bad idea to shake things up from time to time.') And however tragic the momentary existential action – Bowie's Glass Spider Tour or Eric's cowboy boots disaster – the essential cool somchow survives.

Now Eric in turn has himself become a hero, he will in future take his place in the pantheons constructed by others. 'Kill your idols'? Bunch of arse, mate.

L'Homme Sérieux

The cross-Channel adjective 'serious' may well have precisely the same literal meaning to both us and the French but its usage in relation to a man's personality couldn't be more different; in fact, it highlights a distinction Orwell once noted, namely that only in England is 'intellectual' a dirty word – in France, it's the highest accolade, with the possible exceptions of 'good cook' or 'shit-hot in the sack'. Check out that epitome of Brit pop-cultural attitudes, *Blind Date*. The biggest murmur of audience sympathy a post-date girl will get when rejecting the hapless lad she picked is if she says he was 'too serious'. There is no greater social sin than this:

failure to conform to the desired type of the joshing, skitting, joke-cracking self-deprecatory 'good bloke' is fatal. Cherishing the English sense of humour is one of the last values that binds us together, common decency and good manners having disappeared along with Ealing comedies and unlocked front doors. Poking fun and 'having a larf' permeates everything we do: 'seriousness' implies 'too clever by half', a phrase even our dim-witted PM recognizes as signifying regrettable English anti-intellectualism.

For the French, *l'homme sérieux* is a figure of desire for both men and women. That's not to say that they don't like a laugh – any nation that can produce Louis de Funès or indeed Jean Paul Gaultier can hold its own in the trouser-wetting stakes when necessary. But humour doesn't pervade their existence as it does ours. Look at their TV schedules: comedic content is kept entirely separate so as not to infect the serious stuff. Moreover, they get emblazoned with exclamatory overheads like *'Rigolo!'* and *'Pour Rire!'* as if to say 'it's okay France, take off your cool shades for half an hour and have a giggle'. Our cultural icons – Cleese, Sellers, the Beatles, Paxman – are chosen precisely because they take the piss out of the very concept of 'gravitas'; France's are selected for embodying it. And whilst fatuous women's mag surveys here reveal 'a sense of humour' to be a man's most desirable facet, French femininity is opened up by the deeper virtues. As the Provençal saying has it, 'Serious about life, serious about love'; let's face it, when you're getting down to hot slurpy rumpy-pumpy, being able to crack a few Irish jokes isn't going to be much use to you is it?

I'm not saying Eric hasn't got a sense of humour; clearly, as his wonderfully wry post-Cup Final interview demonstrated, he has. But he has never been anything like the stereotypical pro, mucking in with the players' filthy bathtime gag sessions, fooling around with the practical jokers or engaging in the ferocious skitting that the English use to keep each other's heads from swelling. Equally obvious is his refusal to take the classic Anglo-Saxon line on pretentiousness, an attitude exemplified by *Private Eye*'s 'Pseud's Corner' in which an extract from this very book will doubtless one day appear. Instead, he echoes Francis Ford Coppola, interviewed in *Heart Of Darkness*, when he talked of the lethal fear of being accused of pretension; at some point, he argued, 'every true artist has to say f*ck it' – better to aspire to serious art, fail and stand accused than never to reach above oneself at all.'

Eric's quintessential seriousness has alienated some in England, especially within the media who much prefer the easy-going, lad-about-town demeanour of the Gazzas, Sharpes and Fowlers. He is rarely seen with a camera-friendly grin, still less in the frothy banter about shaggin' an' clubbin' that passes for personality profiles in the footie glossies; his punishment for not getting into the English swing of things is to be ridiculed for his 'pretensions'. And it's an effective way of baiting him. Although he affects to find amusing at an intellectual level the piss-taking in *Spitting Image* and *Guignols d'Info*, he doesn't have a record of enjoying being the butt of such attention. Even as a young man at Auxerre, he took exception to others' sardonic mick-taking about his demeanour, dress and accent; still now, when he mentions the current jokes about him, his acceptance of their humorous content is always peppered with quiet protests that he's been misunderstood, that they've missed the point or that their analysis of his attitudes is inaccurate.

The French, however, keep coming back to the altar of Cantona precisely because he is football's *homme sérieux*. Usually, France isn't very forgiving – go there and mention Dunkirk for illustration – and Eric's record of insulting their way of doing things would normally not be forgotten. Yet within weeks of each 'outrage' they are rallying round him once more. *L'Equipe* may well have blared '*Indefensible!*' across its front page of 27 January 1995 but before long public opinion was behind him, portraying Eric as a victim of English xenophobia. As I write, there is a clamour for Eric to be recalled for Euro '96 even though he offended so many with his supposedly bumptious behaviour as French captain in 1994/5. The comparison with attitudes to David Ginola is instructive. Over here, diving apart, Ginola is seen as our kind of Frenchie: the unctuous charm, constant smiles, beach-boy prettiness and self-deprecating humour go down as easily as he does in the penalty box. But in France, Ginola is deeply unpopular; in the Eric–David debate sparked by the French World Cup exit which Cantona blamed on Ginola, the French have reacted on familiar impulse. Remember Henri Leconte, who became the 1980s Ilie Nastase at Wimbledon? How the English loved his clowning humour and devil-may-care flamboyance; never mind that he won sod all. The French were mystified by this: to them, Leconte lacked seriousness. He was a clown, and they didn't mean it as a compliment. They much preferred the dedicated intellectual application and furrowed brow of Guy Forget who made the most of his gifts and won the odd championship: 'Leconte wins the smiles but Forget the points,' as an unwitting punster once remarked at Roland-Garros. In Cantona, the French see what they always wanted: yes, the flair that both they and the English treasure but also the serious craftsman who values gravitas over giggles. The Englishman may well find it easy to laugh at Eric's 'pompous' solemnity but better that than plastic tits and microphone belches, surely?

'House of Style'

The title of the controversial, didactic but immensely amusing fashion and lifestyle column in the fanzine United We Stand. *The brainchild of one particular beautifully threaded Red, it is a focus for every Lauren-worshipping Red in town. Here our expert casts an uncharacteristically self-effacing eye over the Cantona style.*

I'd always lived my life firmly believing in the doctrine of the 1980s casual, that style can only be achieved by purchasing thousands of pounds worth of designer clothing. Then a certain French footballer swaggered into Old Trafford, asked if Manchester United were big enough for him – and all my beliefs were blown out of the water. Here was a man for whom style wasn't something to be acquired but a God-given right. A man who could walk stark naked through the Arndale Centre and still ooze class. A man called Eric Cantona.

Clothes-watchers have always had much to admire in Eric Cantona. After all, his first season in the red shirt ended with him in a beige linen number up on Paco Rabanne's Paris catwalk. Other notable Cantona clobber moments include his smart black single-breasted number which the FA showed no respect for when they dished out an extra ten-match ban for the Simmonds incident; the *très* European blazer and jeans ensemble modelled in the 'Eric The King' video; and, my personal favourite, the Thierry Mugler jacket with grey marl T-shirt worn at the first trial. But if you truly want to understand the Cantona style, it's better to focus on the more eclectic outfits he's graced us with. The zip-up cardie in which Eric faced the press the day after Palace made more Reds question his sanity than had the night before, and the deckchair-stripe jacket with checked shirt which he wore while sitting out the opening game of 1994/5 raised more than the odd bushy eyebrow. If you strutted about the K-Stand concourse wearing this sort of rig you'd probably be accused of making a serious fashion *faux pas*, but Eric just seems to carry it off regardless. When you've got this much style, clothes cease to be important; they're just a means to keep warm. Ryan Giggs, United's resident clothes horse and Armani freak, put it best when he said that Eric is a 'class dresser, he can wear anything and just looks cool'.

So Eric's style goes beyond clothes. It's a way of life which explains his universal appeal for the Red faithful. He plays for United the way you and I would like to, with a snarl, with a swagger, with outrageous confidence in his ability. The patronising Englishman would call it arrogance, I call it belief. Belief that you're the best, that no one can touch you. The kind of belief that leads you to avoid the embarrassing, knicker-wetting celebrations of the Sharpey Shuffle in favour of the proud, statuesque pose that followed his goal against Sheffield United in 1995. The kind of belief that tells you that you can't let anyone take the piss out of your mam, be you in Selhurst or Salford. You'll need to dish out a slap.

If God ever put a cooler man on the planet, I've yet to come across him. Meanwhile I'll keep buzzing off a man whose talent makes opposing defenders weep and whose natural born style means that he can put on dodgy knitwear and still be the King.

Hughesie

Footballers' egos are fragile things. Suggest to some that they owe a significant part of their success to another's efforts and they can bristle, especially if they appear to be carrying the tinges of an inferiority complex. It's faintly amusing that when, for example, either Lee Chapman or Chris Waddle is asked about playing with Eric, the first priority seems to be to minimize and criticize what Eric brought to their respective teams. Yet the simple fact remains that neither Marseilles nor Leeds would have won their titles without Cantona's contribution. From Mark Hughes, there is no such carping. A proud and self-possessed man, he could have taken umbrage at the way Eric rose to dominance over an Old Trafford kingdom Hughesie had thought was his above all. Yet Hughesie's testament is simple, generous and sincere: 'Thank you, Eric Cantona . . . we may not speak the same language but we make the ball talk louder than words. This Frenchman has changed my footballing life.' Of all the United players who thrived on Eric's inspiration, none did so more than Mark Hughes.

Hard to credit in retrospect, but for many observers it was Hughesie's head on the block when Eric arrived. Some said that Hughes and McClair had never really gelled as a partnership; though it was Choccy who had suffered the worst goal drought so far in 1992/3, he had at least been the supporters' player of the year in '92 whereas Hughes was fingered as one of the run-in's disappointments. Never had the siren song that Hughes was impossible to play off been so loudly heard as in those darkest final days of the BC era. But from the moment Ferguson gave Hughes the centre-forward nod ahead of Choccy for the visit of Norwich, Cantona's presence and understanding held the sun high in the sky for Mark Hughes's Indian summer. The effects were instant: as soon as Eric signed Hughes scored six in ten. Leading the line and holding back the opposition dogs of war, he repaid Cantona in kind immediately as Eric floated in behind to score six in his first ten too. Just when Hughes must have felt his career would wind to an end without ever enjoying a true footballing love affair, Eric had given him a bed to share. The cuckolded

Choccy took it very well but then he always was a DIY enthusiast (pass the Kleenex).

So two characters deemed incompatible instead dovetailed into the ultimate focus of United's 4–4–2. As Eric himself noted, he'd worked a similar symbiosis with another unlikely partner, Jean-Pierre Papin: it was all a matter of professional application and intelligence. And rather than them being two 'fireballs waiting to explode' at each other, as Hughes put it, their mutual appreciation of passionate, aggressive competitiveness gave each of them a guaranteed support in times of strife. Whenever Eric hit trouble, Hughes could explain and empathize, often citing the provocation, the lack of protection, the need for fire in the soul – he'd been through the same syndrome. Hughes will always tell you that one key to Red success was that they finally became a 'hard' side. And although he spent much time shielding Eric, 'getting stuck in to let him get on with his stylish football', he approvingly notes that 'Eric could dish it out' with the best of 'em. They were true comrades-in-arms and the battles they won will never be forgotten as long as the Red Flag flies.

'I' is for . . .

Image

It is commonplace these days to remark of any public enterprise, and especially of politics, that reality no longer matters, only the perception. Image over truth, style over substance, means over ends . . . whichever way you cut it, as soon as you step into the arena you're at the mercy of a superficial mentality that is the by-product of the post-modern age. Your only hope is to play the game better than the rest.

The creation and manipulation of Eric's image by himself and others has had wildly variable results; fitting, because he seems to have a typically ambivalent attitude to the whole process. One can't underestimate the power of the ego here: as Eric says, 'I am proud that they talk about me, be it good or bad', in a perhaps conscious echo of the Wildean dictum that the only thing worse than being talked about behind your back is not to be talked about at all. There is also much evidence that playing with personas amuses him. As he's a Bowie fan, you'd expect this, especially when you consider his interest in method acting; indeed, some in France do accuse him of 'inventing' a wolfish character for himself to portray as a counterbalance to his natural shyness and now gloat that he has become imprisoned by his own image.

Personally, I'd suggest that this is far too Machiavellian a view of Eric's motivation. It may well be true, as former team-mate Stéphane Paille reckons, that 'everything you've read and heard about Eric is the opposite of what he's really like'. It is also true that Eric does dabble a little in image-manipulation, playing it up for the cameras and advertisers when necessary, more often than not for a laugh. But fundamentally, the distortion of the Cantona reality is the work of others in the media, not himself. If anything, his view on image-creation is that it is the preserve of politicians, managers and administrators to be 'sufficiently smooth to disguise all of their emotions'. After all, hasn't he always said that he has no interest in acquiring that particular, McCartneyesque talent for pleasing people? Hasn't his credo always been to express his instinct and to hell with the consequences of the image it produces? Furthermore, he has explicitly made the connection between the false image created for him and the fact that this image is then used as a 'role model' for others. Not that he appreciates this role – he vehemently disavows it whenever possible – but he knows that whatever he may say, there are people out there who fall for it.

The truth is that Cantona has long since abandoned any hope of controlling his image. He is the opposite of the Mandelsonian Labour Party: he cares little now for how things are seen, only for the reality as it affects his family and club. That is why he declares simply that 'I don't attach any importance to what people say at my expense'. They are reacting to a perception, an image, an illusion; he hasn't the time to bother with those so susceptible to the shallowest judgements. That is why he maintained a stoic silence throughout the trials of 1995 and never stoops to PR tabloid puff-pieces and self-justificatory interviews. In political terms, he looks after the policy and lets the minions take care of the spin-doctoring, a pleasantly old-fashioned reversal of current practice and all the more welcome for it.

The Inner Child

One of the most depressing features of the Selhurst Park fall-out was the opportunistic and grubby way the media used children, whether it was through printing pics of supposedly traumatized kids in the family stand or by whipping up hysteria over Eric becoming a terrible role model: it helped portray Cantona as virtually a bug-gery short of being a child abuser. Both approaches were fundamentally bollocks, of course. Those kids in the stand, whose dads filled the tabloids with their bleating, will dine out on their eyewitness accounts for the rest of their lives. I bet most of them couldn't wait to get to the playground to boast next day. I'd swap their eight-year-olds' 'trauma' for mine – the 1976 Cup Final – any day. As for Eric being a role model, what example had he set? That if you lash out, you get punished beyond all normal proportion; what better line for a teacher to spin to a young bully than to threaten him with a dose of the Kelly 'n' Pearch treatment? ('If you hurt little

Jenny again, it'll be two weeks in the plimsoll cupboard and no Nintendo for ten months, me laddo.') The irony is that Eric's love of children – and, more importantly, his respect and admiration for the purity of childhood – is one of his most appealing features.

The question of role models can be easily dealt with by quoting my favourite passage from Eric's own book, a ringing declaration of progressivism that deserves to be shouted in the face of Nick Tate, Gillian Shephard and all those imported 'communitarian' crypto-fascists:

> I think one should stop treating the heart and soul of youngsters as clay to be modelled in whatever fashion you like. I am not there to educate anyone; I don't see that as my 'role'. They should be able to work things out for themselves. Children go where they find sincerity and authenticity. In my way of working, I don't betray anybody and they know it. I don't consider that it would be better to teach them to deny their own emotions for the benefit of the established order. Is it in teaching people to be sub-missive that they become adult citizens?

Generally speaking, the French don't take kindly to lectures from the English about how to relate to kids in the first place. They say of us that we treat animals better than children – compare the incomes of the NSPCC and the RSPCA for illustration – and view our bourgeoisie's habit of getting rid of the brats by signing them up to a life of brutality in public schools as typical. Conversely, the biggest English grumbling you'll hear on a Côte d'Azur beach is how indulgent French parents are with their children; what we term running wild the French see as youthful self-expression. Complain to a Parisian dad that his darlings just demolished your sandcastle and he'll tell you it was valid architectural criticism.

So Eric is scarcely the ogre with our kids, quite the opposite. Loath though I am to quote the Establishment's advocate David Meek, he has pointed out that Eric is the most solicitous of all the pros with kids. After training, many players will plot an escape or try and scrawl one or two signatures before shooting off. Eric will work his way through the crowd of imploring fans, stopping to sign for every one, chatting to them as best he can, often not leaving until an hour later. Similarly, while many superstars leave the meet-the-disabled-kid 'chores' behind them when they've made it, for lesser players to do, have you noticed how often Eric is on hand to do the honours? And he is reported to have said, following his community service 'punishment', that what would have been a drag for others was one of the most fulfilling experiences he'd ever had. He was back in the world of children, which he once said he wished he'd never had to leave.

I once put this to a cynic who scoffed 'So what? Adolf Hitler loved animals and children too.' (He is a Chelsea fan, and consequently a Hitler expert.) Taking on board this frenziedly inappropriate comparison, the sort in which the ABU brigades specialize, the point is that Cantona still believes in the purity of childhood. In some senses, to rejig a phrase, he has *not* put away childish things. He still speaks of listening to his inner child because that was when he was at his most uncorruptedly instinctive and spontaneous; that is the nature he seeks to preserve. 'There is no finer childhood than that which is balanced between sport and the imaginary,' he once remarked, and though he now plays his football in a money-dominated environment rather than the innocent Caillols streets, the time left for make-believe and imagination now much less than it was, there is still a sense as in Houllier's words that he remains exactly like the 'precocious gifted child of the family'. Temper tantrums and playground scraps included. (>> Spontaneity, *Weltanschauung*)

Inter Milan

The bane of every English fan's life is the Continental predator. Bad enough having any number of lithe and lissom locals swimming around our women folk, promising them superior technique and finishing power when we're on our hols, but it's too much to have their dodgy agents piling through the Eurotunnel, laden with lire or pesetas, in search of prime English beef. English players, like our girls, are easy heads to turn. No self-respecting pro can feel he's arrived until the *Daily Scum* has carried some agent-supplied speculation that he's a target for Atletico this or Sporting that. If they fall for it, it almost always ends in tears as they're used, abused and dumped back in Blighty with several knee injuries and a king-sized attitude problem. Suitors go in and out of style: in the late 1970s the Germans were cool, in the 1980s the Spanish, and even for a time in the 1990s

France was the place to be seen. The one constant, however, has been the omnipresent lurking menace of the Italians, ever ready to pinch both your wife's bum and your club's best player.

The Italians, and in particular the Milanese, have had their eye on Eric since 1988, at least. When he moved to Marseilles, Silvio Berlusconi made a last-minute attempt to snatch him for AC – Eric could have been in the vanguard of that outstanding Dutch-influenced European Cup side. These days, since Signor Moratti took over at Inter, it's been the inferior San Siro cohabitees who've been sniffing around. Three separate, definite bids have so far been tabled and refused by either player or club; as long as Eric remains a contender the threat will never be dispelled, even if they may currently pretend to be uninterested.

Eric has always been quite honest about the appeal of the Italian Job. He knows that whatever the Sky/Premier League hypemeisters say, Italy remains the chosen arena for Europe's best gladiators. He recalls how Michel Platini succeeded there and proved himself as the world's premier playmaker, and he cannot be immune to the cultural banquet Italy's great renaissance cities offer him. As long as Paul Ince stays at Inter, there is a special personal pull too, not to mention the knowledge that he would be protected come what may as one of Moratti's protégés. Yet he has also freely admitted that the Italian way would present difficulties. Who would want to sacrifice the open spaces, thrilling tempo and easily defeated English donkey defenders for the cramped, assassin-dominated killing fields of an Italian pitch? Whatever the balance of argument in Cantona's mind, one thing is certain: he has never ruled it out as inconceivable. If Eric does leave for that final, irresistible challenge – and Reds have come face to face with the prospect twice already – then barring some calamity he will do so with every Red's blessing. That was the commonest response during the last panic attack: so long and thanks for all the fish. The paradox is that Cantona leaving is every Red's worst nightmare, yet also the eventuality for which we are most prepared. However much it will hurt, it is of course always better to have loved and lost than never to have loved at all.

Isabelle

All right, so this is an appallingly crass way of putting it, but what a lucky dog Eric was at seventeen. Not only did a bloke turn up at work with whom he could be laddish best mates – they went on the piss together for a year and generally lived it up – but the guy had an eminently fanciable, Cantona-compatible sister too. Bernard 'Nino' Ferrer joined Eric at Auxerre in the late summer of 1983 and soon introduced him to his svelte, intelligent and sophisticated older sister Isabelle. Three years Cantona's senior and already a university literature scholar at Aix-en-Provence, she put down a marker for Eric to pick up when he was ready; as yet, he still had a few oats to sow and magnums to drain. But by the time the pair met again at Nino's wedding in 1985 Eric had matured, his national service done and a serious football career now an assured prospect. At nineteen and twenty-two, the pair were now very much 'game on'.

A few weeks later, Isabelle came over to spend a fortnight at Eric's pad which he has described as the most magical of his life: I think we can read between the lines here. He tells of an aborted farewell at Auxerre station when the two couldn't bear to separate; the way he recounts it summons up the fabulous white-out plat-form sequence at the finale of *Un Homme Et Une Femme*. It may, as Eric remarked, have been an exit from Bohemia for him but it was certainly the entrance to Elysium.

Guy Roux, as adorably as ever, played his matchmaker role to perfection, stitching up a loan to Martigues for Eric so that he could go and live in a cramped but romantic studio flat with Isabelle in Aix. He was clearly resigned to the fact that in the first flush of rampant infatuation he wouldn't be much use to Auxerre away from his new soul-mate, not to mention the likelihood that he would be permanently shagged-out. Together they lived out the cliché of never poorer, never happier, and as they roved around the countryside in his battered Peugeot from one romantic rendezvous to another, Eric, by his admission, 'forgot about football completely: the world could have crumbled at our door'.

Now approaching a decade of marriage with two beautiful kids to show for it, they remain a rarity in football marriages. Isabelle is scarcely the archetypal football wife, being a respected academic in her own right and by all accounts not the sort of woman to follow meekly in her husband's path. Eric's rueful account of her response to Selhurst Park, metaphorically waving the rolling pin, says something, as does her apparent centrality in all his professional decision-making. And there is little doubt that her influence has been a major contribution in keeping Eric true to himself. He often speaks of her indifference to money and disdain for flash lifestyles, and is proud that they 'have never abandoned the values that have earned us the right to hold our heads up high'. To her, 'a good book is always more valuable than a nice car', a comparison which speaks volumes for the way the Cantonas see the spiritual and material in life. Now if she could only see her way to letting the next Cantona male sprog be born in England . . .

'J' is for . . .

Jason Davies

The mid-Cheshire Red who battles through home and away on crutches. Widely credited with being an originator of the '90s standard 'Fergie's Red And White Army', he can be found wherever Eric-worshippers congregate bellowing passionately for our God and Club.

How we hated Cantona. Just days after he had won the League for the Leeds scum virtually single-handedly, he had sent the sheep-molesters into the orgasmic mode usually spared for Flossy in the field with the words 'I don't know why I love you but I do'. However we were later to discover, courtesy of our own *Red Issue*, that his English wasn't quite up to scratch; what he actually meant was 'I hate it here and I am going to move to the greatest team in the world as soon as boring Wilko lets me go'. And there was us thinking he really did care for the Munich-singing, plane-impersonating, Flossy-f*cking inbreds that like to tell us 'we are Leeds and proud of it'.

Then one strange November day later that year, we ended up signing the *enfant terrible* from under the bastards' very noses. And what a f*cking laugh we had at the sight of all the Leeds fans going mental because we, Man U, had signed the best player they had seen there in years. He was now ours – from French Twat to Mon Dieu. The fact that he eventually won us the title, as he had with Leeds the year before, was just an added bonus. We couldn't help but think of the bitter and twisted state of the YRA down the road crying in their sheep dip. Bliss.

For some Reds, it was hard to accept him at first. Before his debut against the Bittermen, I heard comments like 'I won't be singing that sheep-shagger's name', as if the thought of TV-watching Leeds fans wallowing in self-pity and Red-loathing wasn't cause enough to warrant some praise. But we were about to find out what a genius he is, from his 'superb overhead kicks to his remarkable backflicks' (and kung-fu). He is still, and will be for ever, Our King.

Jean Jacques Rousseau

If you're seriously interested in 'La Philosophie de Cantona', then you'll need more than the Megastore's £4.99 random selection of quotes which have been chucked together under that title. Fortunately Eric has provided enough evidence, not only explicitly in his interviews but also in the significantly familiar language and phrases he uses, for us to be able to piece together the philosophical development he's undergone and propose a unifying hypothesis. (>> Existential Eric, the Inner

Child, Spontaneity, Family Values, 'Lodger', *Weltan-schauung*, Zodiac)

It's fitting that Eric is often dubbed a 'romantic' in the everyday sense of the word because eighteenth-century Romanticism as a concept is the best place to start. And the greatest of the early Romantic thinkers, cited by both Eric and his detractors as a key influence, was Jean Jacques Rousseau. Just in terms of personality, there are familiar echoes: Rousseau stomped about mid-century Europe from city to city, never satisfied with the status quo, prone to the emotional outbursts which his love of instinctivism encouraged. (He even had a parallel experience to the Wilko-Canto episode, going into exile to shack up with the level-headed David Hume whom he drove to distraction with his temperamental behaviour. No recorded kung-fu incidents, however.) But it is Rousseau's works, in particular his novels *La Nouvelle Héloise*, *Emile* and the classic treatise *Du Contrat Social*, that have had such an impact on Eric; you will surely recognize the following beliefs from countless Cantona quotes. The first principle is that Original Sin is a bogus concept (apologies to unlapsed Catholics here) – man is born naturally good with innate liberty and nobility, hence the groovy catchphrase 'Noble Savage'. But, as the famous opening of *The Social Contract* has it, 'men are born free, yet everywhere they are in chains'. The free being is corrupted and imprisoned by urban conditions, class hierarchy and governmental tyranny; the good natural man is made bad by absolutist arbitrary institutions that rob him of his powers.

The Jean Jacques/Eric ideal, most visible in Rousseau's early novels and in Cantona's views on education, the pastoral life and the importance of instinct, recognizes that although the romantic is a suffering, solitary observer of an unjust world, there is still a route to salvation that doesn't rely on society. Man's natural liberty and nobility can be preserved and developed through self-expression, discarding ponderous reason and self-restraint in favour of acting upon emotion and sentiment. This can only work for the good if your education has been one of liberation rather than constraint; especially in *Emile*, Rousseau commends an education that develops inherently good moral sentiments by teaching through experience and the direct influence of people rather than via books and theory. To him, the family rather than the school should be the prime mover, and in championing empathy over punishment I suppose you could label him the first 'trendy teech', in modern tabloid vernacular.

Naturally, this is hopeless if the environment you grow up in is already riddled with moral corruption, but Eric's was famously idyllic. Reading about his early life reveals that his family, and in particular his father, were as noble and free as any Rousseauesque ideal could require. And switching Romantics for a moment, if Wordsworth's ideal was of a unity between the self and 'Nature' unencumbered by intervening social artifice, then Eric's love for the countryside inculcated by his father has proved to be an enduring value in itself as well as a metaphor for his absolute determination to stay true to his own personality's nature. Just as Rousseau is a first-base point from which wildly differing modes of thought have veered off in all directions, from Herder to Hegel and Shelley to Sartre, the importance of this stuff relates mainly to Cantona as a child and teenager. It's about developing what is within and discovering 'who you are' in a pure, undistorted environment which, above all, allows you to understand and preserve your freedom. But what then? As you step out into the wider world, you know your characteristics – it's what you make of them that matters now. (>> Existential Eric)

Julius Caesar

The time will surely come when Eric will be upgraded from King to Emperor, preferably after a Red Army invasion of the Continent brings home the Champions Cup and Eric takes his rightful place as the colossus bestriding Europe. We can but dream . . . And who better for historical parallel than Julius Caesar? Phenomenally gifted, both a Creator and Destroyer, a respected artist and a man of unparalleled tactical vision (let's leave aside any Kubrickian notions of homosexuality though). Both, however, were brought low by the rabid jealousy and plotting of others, of inferior mortals unable to cope with imperial grandeur and glamour. 'Beware the Ides of March' said the soothsayer to Caesar, and so too with Eric, thrice in recent times under assault during dark mid-March days. In '92, his first Leeds crisis, with Wilko cast as Brutus; in '95, the Inter vultures circled as Eric went into court-room battle with the crazed magistocracy. And here we remember March '94 when the world gave us Reds a taste of what was to come.

Looking into the entrails of previous United victims, any decent soothsayer could have seen it coming. At Norwich, an unpunished studs-up assault on Eric had clearly enraged him to the point where he exacted a mild revenge on both the perpetrator and the next Canary to cross him. His personal justice code had operated in the absence of any other, but Jimmy Hill and Co. were unimpressed, spluttering outrage across the airwaves. How grateful they must have been that Eric had provided their TV coverage with a newsquake and didn't they make the most of it? At Wimbledon, Eric chose simply to embarrass those who attempted to lunge at his precious limbs but remained unhappy with the lack of official protection. Perhaps it was inevitable that the next miscreant would receive the full Imperial Stamp of Disapproval.

Swindon was a weird day out. A tinpot club who'd dreamed all season about this match decided to stage it as a Leeds '71 revival. Fans who'd never encountered us before spat venom and, well, spat at us as if we were deadly rivals. Munich songs abounded, coaches were encircled; at one point Hughes was struck by a local cretin from the crowd. (Imagine the police search: Wanted – Local assailant. Description – hideous yokel accent and minuscule IQ. Suspects – About 20,000?) Swindon players combined some fairly intelligent play with an array of shirt-pulls, tugs and sly knocks in best old-Tyke style. When Eric snapped midway through the second-half, it was the classic existentialist response to the absurd world of injustice.

It wasn't actually that bad a stamping, more of a

theatrical tread; looking at Eric's leg musculature, one can imagine his full force bringing forth geysers of guts and intestine. Maybe it was the complete transparency and honesty of it that shocked. There was no attempt at disguise or justification, no sneaky wait for a referee's averted gaze, just the instinctive rage of an artist rejecting society's codes of normality. Perhaps Van Gogh was in a similar kind of bate when he cut his own ear off? 'Typical Dutchman', Lawrie Sanchez would no doubt have sneered.

With tabloid newsprint supplies not yet exhausted, there was room left for yet more triple-page spreads four days later after Eric stalked off at Highbury. The fact that the second yellow card for innocently colliding with Winterburn was patently unjustified scarcely mattered. Even Arsenal players coming to Eric's defence was deemed suitable only for tenth paragraph asides. A Royal Pardon would not have been enough to deflect the tabloid mission to plunge the dagger into Caesar's back. After all, they had waited many months for this chance to demonstrate that the self-appointed experts had been right from the off – this 'Gallic' was trouble, too arrogant and too individualist. A five-match ban, dubbed 'lenient' by the rope-twirling lynch-mob, might as well have been seven, for a wounded Eric was not all there at Wembley and against Liverpool. He would later return in a Julian Triumph, the jackanapes bound in chains behind him; but we had all witnessed a chilling exhibition of what lay in wait for Eric next time he transgressed the codes of conformity. (>> Venue of Legends)

'K' is for . . .

King of Old Trafford

'**E**ric The King'; now the most commonplace of clichés but still testament to a most special honour. For the last undisputed Red King was Denis Law; since then there may have been Captain Marvels, Merlins and Guv'nors but none has quite lifted the Lawman's old crown. But on 11 September 1993, on the open end at Chelsea, a burly Burnage Boy with a burgeoning reputation as a terrace songsmith led around a dozen acolytes through the first public airing of 'Eric The King', the words to which he'd invented in his bath and later typed up for his mates. As he finished, the hundred or so lads around burst into applause. A terrace classic had been born and with it, a new King crowned.

Approval for players comes from all quarters. There are the pros' pros, the pundits' favourites, the managers' pets, but true immortality is bestowed on the fans' heroes. They are the players whose legendary deeds will be recounted from generation to generation of supporter; for the man on the pitch, can anything compare with the roaring worship of 45,000? And as few supporters are fortunate enough to have access to the public

platforms of the media, the one sure method of expressing their collective will is through the terrace song.
Judged on these terms, Eric is arguably the most popular
Red of our time. At first, Old Trafford resorted to the
obvious 'Ooh-Ah Cantona' to the Odyssey tune, a
straight steal from Leeds but with a Red parentage from
Paul McGrath's glory days. An adapted *Marseillaise* soon
followed, wordless until the final 'Ooh-Ahs', still an
inspiring, almost haunting sound; then, when Go West
fever arrived from Italy, Eric's name was the first to be
inserted. New Year's Day, 1994: Leeds are silenced by a
deafening volley of our Yuletide hit 'The Twelve Days Of
Cantona', a song reliant on the same amusingly absurd
repetition as the George Best 'Yellow Submarine' adap-
tation and now sung with no regard to the seasonal
topicality. And for the connoisseurs, there's Boylie's
'What a Friend' and 'Monsieur Genius', featured on the
first album ever devoted to just one footballer.

But it is 'Eric The King' that remains the ultimate
expression of fan devotion. A growing hit throughout
United's triumphant 1994 Cup run, it has now become
the one genuine terrace classic (re)invented during the
1990s – aptly inspired by a 1968 Law chant. No one
who was there will forget that fabulous Red night out
at Vale Park in 1994 when every old favourite got an
airing; the *pièce de résistance*, however, was the full version of 'Eric The King'. Three thousand, crammed under
the roof at one end enjoying the acoustics, maintained
total silence as Pete's boys bellowed the verses across the
terraces before coming in *en masse* for ripping choruses.
'Pete Boyle & The K-Standers' went on to have a major

indie hit with the 'Eric The King' single, appeared live on breakfast TV, provided the soundtrack to Eric's court appearances and made an album – but only once they'd received the regal blessing. So for those who still haven't caught the Boylie vibe, here's your introduction: the lyrics to two Cantona classics.

ERIC THE KING
(to the tune 'Lily The Pink')

Chorus:
WE'LL . . . DRINK A DRINK A DRINK
TO ERIC THE KING, THE KING, THE KING
HE'S THE LEADER OF OUR FOOTBALL TEAM
HE'S THE GREATEST FRENCH FOOTBALLER
THAT THE WORLD HAS EVER SEEN

Eric The King, he's remarkably trendy,
He's done some modelling around town
Wearing the best suits up on the catwalk
Whilst the Leeds scum they just frown.
On the field, it's almost unreal
Some of the things that Eric does:
Superb overhead kicks, remarkable back flicks,
I'm sure the guy just takes the piss.

He once played for Marseille but never for Arsenal
Or Liverpool or even Man City;
Landed in Yorkshire, a terrible blunder,
Which was ten months with the Sheep;
He had his brief spell there with the Leeds scum
But then he realized that they were has-beens,
Only one way now for Eric to go now
To the Theatre of all Dreams.

Eric is so cool, remarkably cultured,
He likes good music and poetry too,
Performing the fine arts on the field
For the boys they call Man U.
He is a legend without any doubt,
He will reign for years to come;
We will just stand there in admiration
With countless more trophies won.

The end of November, we'll always remember
As the time he made that special move:
Poetry in motion, the deadliest potion,
He's got nothing left to prove.
The King's still our hero, as well as De Niro,
But this ain't movies this is real life.
He won't leave United, for that we're delighted
Because this club's his perfect wife.

© Peter Boyle 1993

MONSIEUR GENIUS
(to the tune 'I'd like to teach...')

(Spoken intro in Irish accent):
This song is not a rebel song,
This song is not a protest song,
. . . this song is an Eric song.

We've come to watch Eric the King, the genius of the land,
He's French and flash, a different class,
He makes the whole ground stand.
The master of the football arts
The rest are also-rans,
Oh Cantona, the King by far,
The idol of the fans.

He makes us stand, we chant his name,
We sing the *Marseillaise*;
He is the King, he's everywhere,
Welcome back those glory days.

© Peter Boyle 1995

(Full band versions of these and other Eric epics are available on *Cantona The Album*: tel. Jim on 0181 299 2342 for details.)

Kung-Fu Fighting

And so to the moment of madness, the resurrection of Bruce Lee, the defining image of the season or whatever other label you like. Reds at Selhurst Park were still taking their post-lavatorial seats when a ball from our left looped limply over the heads of Eric and his marker / assassin Richard Shaw. Seconds earlier, Shaw had fouled Eric for the third time and gone unpunished once more. As the ball passed by, Eric extended a mildly petulant leg which, if it actually caught Shaw, could have done no more harm than a breath of summer breeze. Shaw appeared to hesitate, mid-air, for several seconds before apparently realizing that the Oscar season was upon us.

Our stand was imbued with resignation rather than shock. After all, it had been six months since Eric's last dismissal and our knowledge of English refs is such that we knew a red card was well overdue. We watched from a position directly opposite as Eric traipsed down the touchline with Norm 'Munster' Davies in half-hearted pursuit. If only he'd set off alongside him . . . Everyone I've spoken to since had their eyes fixed on Eric. We saw what the TV cameras missed and what few cameras captured. Some lone lout, hardly the type that's supposed to be in a family stand, hurtles several rows down to the front. His nastily naff leather jacket is unmistakable from even seventy yards – we are watching a creature from low down the food chain. He crosses 'the line' – not necessarily a physical mark on the ground but that boundary which we all recognize, the one that separates the players' universe from ours. He's in the 'no man's land' behind the hoardings, as close to the pitch as is possible without actually invading it, yet still a location in which a fan's presence would guarantee official intervention at any other ground. From our vantage point, he appears to be leaning over, inches from Cantona's face. He could be carrying a knife or bottle but a steward feet away does nothing. Someone shouts near me, 'What's he throwing?' To us, it looks as though some sort of attempted assault is in preparation – but by the lout, not Eric. Norm chugs up at last, pulling Eric away and we think, 'It's all over' . . . then something snaps within the mind of the genius and a hundred front pages are born. You've seen the rest.

For someone who's supposed to be a historian with a sense of the importance of events, it's a poor do to have to admit that I didn't really grasp the implications of Eric's actions until leaving the stand. Brooding on the lost points, pausing to watch the pack of Reds who hared down the hill to sort out a Palace mob, I was startled to hear a pair of Dwaynes discussing Eric's prospects using phrases such as 'life ban'. Only then, as police horses in the background clattered towards the warring fans yards away, did it strike me what the world would make of Eric's pugilistics. With battling Reds scarpering from the police in all directions, I reflected that the time for fighting had passed – somewhere out there under the London night sky, the media would be preparing a gallows.

'L' is for . . .

Leisure

Let's face it: being a footballer is frankly a bit of a doss. Ninety minutes' concentrated work a week with the occasional mid-week overtime and the odd runabout for a couple of hours every morning. Surely only backbench MPs and the royal spongers have it easier. Remarkable, then, that so many players seem to make so little use of their endless leisure time. Typical was one United player interviewed on a video: a young man with the world at his feet and limitless capital, his major complaint was that he 'got bored rattling around the house with nothing to do'. Sometimes youth is truly wasted on the young.

Eric, however, has a proper hinterland. There is his love of literature and serious biography; he has the shelves stuffed with classics like any upwardly mobile man but he has actually read and re-read his, Pagnol's works being the most well-thumbed. Like many modern Frenchmen of the *Cahiers du Cinéma* era, his appreciation of film is at a critical, studious level which many Brits would find alien; fortunately, he has the excellent Cornerhouse on Manchester's Oxford Road to satiate his more exotic desires. Indeed, if you're out on a Cantona-hunt, the rather nasty bar attached to the art-house is a good place to check although it is said his visits are less frequent following an unpleasant incident there with Eric-baiters in 1995. And quintessential Frenchman that he is, his gastronomic interest survives among a nation characterized by his countrymen as the food hell of the world; several Wilmslow Road establishments have been stunned by sudden visitations although his favourite remains a particular French cuisine specialist which should remain unnamed lest any Bitters are reading. He will even occasionally fall into line with the lads and cut a rug or two at Home or the Haç, fortified with a drink or two at Cheerleaders, though his major roistering days are well behind him. After all, he is married to a strong woman and has two kids to dote upon; and besides, like a good Euro pro, he is rather more careful about his alcohol intake than some other dressing-room swiggers we could mention.

But that is the urban Cantona; there is no doubt that his spirit is pastoral. Only in the countryside can he get back in touch with his idyllic childhood existence and take part in the pastimes taught to him by his father: hunting and painting. Only there too can he truly discover an escape from the pressures of city life: 'The silence of the countryside has always been indispensable to me. The calm of nature precedes and follows the storm at the stadium. I have always needed such a contrast.' His painting is perhaps his most important outlet: 'It wasn't just an apprenticeship in painting that I received – it was also another way of looking at the world.' As we shall see (>> *Weltanschauung*), painting has indeed had a dominant influence on the way he sees his role as a sportsman. The works themselves are generally abstracts, marked by a brilliant use of colour that must have been shaped by his childhood Marseilles school favourites; Eric says of them that 'they express my dreams, fears, anguish and power'. Since they threaten to reveal more about him than words ever could, let's hope we don't have to wait until the Lowry Centre is built before we have a chance to see them exhibited. Perhaps the Whitworth could give him a ring?

'Lodger'

The most underrated of Bowie's classic Eno trilogy; together with the extraordinary title track from *Station To Station*, it 'celebrates' the rootless, ever-shifting existence of the voyager. Some say Eric prefers *Hunky Dory* but I don't believe it. This was the most explicit expression of the 1970s Bowie credo yet: search, change, challenge yourself, but never stand still. As the centre-piece 'Move On' suggests, it isn't what you're looking for that matters but the value of the journey in itself. Even now he never lets promises of performance be extracted, preferring only metaphors of life as a voyage; like so many wandering heroes of existentialist novels, he knows that one's freedom is tested and extended only through movement and new situations. To stay still is to risk atrophy and the hideous, smothering embrace of cosy conformity. Look no further than Bowie himself: once he'd made a final statement of sorts with *Scary*

Monsters, that was it – Iman, slippers and wallpaper design was all that he had left.

If the nomadic spirit resurfaces, we can't say we weren't warned; as Eric has said: 'Whatever club I'm playing for, wherever I'm living, I never think of myself as a permanent fixture . . . I say to myself, I am just passing through . . . I am proud of playing for United but I must say again that I am on a journey . . . It's important to have been places, for yourself and for your relationship with others.' Cantona's wanderlust, which he suspects runs in a family who are all exiles of sorts, was apparent from an early age; it was an obvious expression of a love for liberty and his intellectual curiosity. Yet equally he was intensely attached to both his family and his region and not just because of his youth – he has pined for both with regularity throughout adulthood, the longing of the inner child only lessened as he has established his own family and found a familial club. But as a teenager, he made the choice, almost forcing himself to accept freedom and a commitment to football, conscious that his own father had been unable to satiate his own desire to travel and discover. 'I was abandoning all that I had loved ever since I could remember,' he later remarked, but in doing so he became a free man, existentially free and therefore at liberty later to choose to maintain the values he had been taught. Marxists, in another context, talk of 'false consciousness'; here that would suggest Eric might have been too irrevocably shaped by his upbringing ever to be able to make a clear judgement. But surely, by choosing a physical freedom

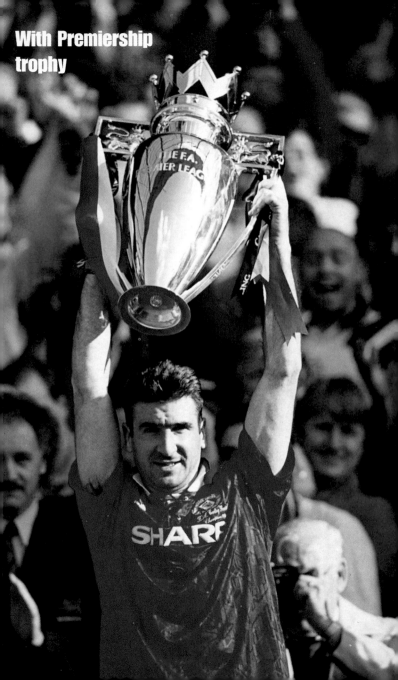

With Premiership trophy

With Leeds

With France

Felled by Tony
Adams's tackle

Charity Shield 1992 – Cantona celebrates

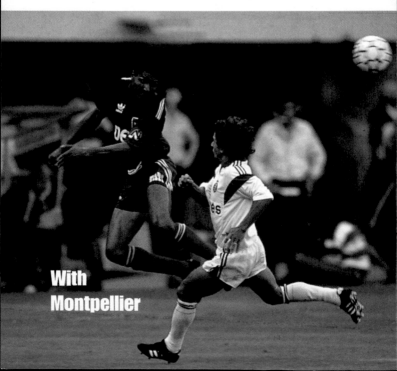

With Montpellier

Throw-in

With Steve Bruce

Overhead strike

at fifteen, he also secured his intellect's *Road To Freedom*. (>> Spontaneity, the Inner Child)

Loot

He may not look it as he steps out of any of his succession of humble homes into a runabout car dressed in casual threads, but Eric is majorly minted. Depending on which tabloid guess you read and how the signing fees and bonuses are calculated, he pulls in somewhere between £15,000 and £20,000 a week. Only Andy Cole's package is supposed to come anywhere near it. Sporadically, the press attempt to whip up some good old-fashioned class-hatred envy over this, but when the bottom-line figure briefly appeared to be a bone of contention during the 1995 contract talks, the response from most Reds I talked to was quite the opposite. One even seriously suggested we volunteer to pay a ticket-price 'Cantona levy' to make up any shortfall. However much he gets – and it works out at a trivial seventy-five pence per match-going head – the consensus is that he's worth every penny. And however much he made from Old Trafford last year, remember that one man took even more – Martin Edwards. I think I know whose performance-related pay constitutes the better value . . .

The endless media fascination with superstar pay-packets is intensely tedious. To me, anyone earning over £1,000 a week is a rich lucky bastard – beyond that, what are a few noughts between friends? All Premiership players are loaded: so what? Who has a more legitimate claim to the money that pours in than the performers themselves? Eric has never had any doubts as to the morality here: 'A footballer earns the money he deserves. Singers and actors earn millions and have the same public. Like them, we have a right to be respected.' So far, so fair: and better the red-shirted heroes become millionaires off our backs than the boardroom fat-cats.

But Eric's attitude to money has developed beyond the simple language of reward and entitlement. For the fact remains that, as much as he earns, he doesn't appear to spend very much of it. Bluntly, he doesn't live on Millionaires' Row and shows no sign of ever wanting to. At the time of his megadosh move to Olympique Marseilles he remarked that the money in itself was meaningless; it's what the offer of it signified that mattered. He has talked often of the terrible corruption of football by money and, more precisely, the money-men; he is now resigned to the dominance of the dollar. So for Eric the bottom-line game is important in two respects. Firstly, if football's administrators want to reckon everything up in fiscal terms, so be it: that must therefore involve massive payments to the stars. Once a club has sacrificed itself to Mammon, they have forfeited the right to talk of playing for the honour of the jersey and so forth. Secondly, now that football has reduced the notion of a player's value to a purely monetary expression, how else can he understand how much he is valued by the club? It's no use sweet-talking a player and heaping him with garlands if you're not prepared to prove it in the language which you have decreed really matters. Eric has, it seems, understood the black cynical soul at the heart of football; but if that's the game, he'll play it with the best.

Perhaps that approach still dispirits some, but there are two mitigating factors. As Eric himself noted, 'Fools are convinced that a footballer goes only where the money is. If they don't want to die ignorant they should realize that there are other issues which form part of the negotiations.' Inter Milan have offered more than once to double Eric's money, showing their desire in the only way that matters, yet Eric has chosen to stay. What was important was that United went as high as they felt able whereas had Eric joined Inter, there would still have been a couple of players on more. That is evidence, reminiscent of the biblical parable about the charity of rich and poor, that it's not money itself but what it signifies that matters to Eric. Secondly, imagine how much he could be making if he was prepared to prostitute himself as much as MUFC has. Sure he has his couple of deals, but such is the demand for Cantona endorsements, interviews and appearances, he could make double his salary off the field if he chose to and would be more omnipresent than Giggs and Sharpe combined. That he has left this potential gold seam virtually unmined says everything about both his self-respect and his essential indifference to money itself. (>> 'U or Non-U?')

Losing

One of the more loathsome legacies bequeathed by the
nineteenth-century public school sporting élite is
the cult of the 'good loser'. How did England ever
become so enraptured by this effete concept? The pam-
pered aristocracy could obviously afford such niceties in
defeat because they possessed so many other privileges
that the odd lost battle didn't mean much. The further
down the pyramid you go, the less defeat can be so
mitigated; when any given struggle is over the only
meaningful feature of your life, you lose badly – and
rightly so. The Edwardian upper classes may have tut-
tutted over *The Times* as they read reports of the first
football hooligans rioting after lost Cup finals, but when
your club was the most important thing in your life apart
from six days in the factory then being a 'good loser'
was hardly an attractive model.

There is a revealing unpublished passage about this
in the exclusive Bernard Morlino interview with Eric
that features in *United We Stood*. The subject of modern
Olympic founder Pierre Coubertin comes up and Eric
bristles as he repeats the infamous maxim about 'the
important thing is the taking part, not the winning'.
Bernard suggests that it has been misinterpreted –
Coubertin meant to say that he wanted all races and
creeds to join in, not that winning didn't matter.
Eric points out that the damage has been done: 'This
misinterpretation is the greatest scandal in sport . . .
sportsmen shelter behind it as an excuse. So Coubertin
meant to say "give everyone a chance". What that does

not mean is "play the final, and if you lose, so what?" '

Clearly, as you would expect from a man of passion, Eric could never be one of those 'good loser' pros to whom defeat means little more than the loss of a win bonus.

The days when Eric used to rip apart bats and tables when he lost at ping-pong are long gone, but it's obvious that it takes him a long time to get over an important defeat. Judging by the number of times he mentions them, the most painful seem to have been the national team's exits from the 1994 World Cup and Euro '92, as well as the repeated failures of his club sides to make proper progress in Europe. As we have seen, a mere French Cup defeat once dispirited him enough to tip him over the edge and demand transfer to any place where such an experience would be rarer (>> *Bonjour Tristesse*).

So, like most United fans I know, Eric will never be equanimous in defeat. But as Steve Black, whose exhibition of raging unsportsmanship at Upton Park last year cheered everyone up immensely, remarked in *As The Reds Go Marching On*, the catharsis of both victory and defeat is good for the soul, and there are no highs without the lows. Eric's on the same wavelength when he remarks: 'To achieve happiness, you sometimes have to go through the worst steps of despair. Genius is about digging yourself out of the hole you've fallen or been pushed into. Failures make you succeed.' So Wembley 1991 begat Wembley 1992; the 1992 title race that of 1993; and perhaps Nou Camp 1994 will teach us for San Siro 1996? For as Shakespeare concludes in *As You Like It*, 'sweet are the uses of adversity'.

'M' is for . . .

Matt Busby

For Eric, as for us all, 1993/4 was the *annus mirabilis*. To take us to emotional heights on a similar plane to those of May 1993 was the tallest of orders; by winning the Double and producing football of such extravagant purity, the King and his knights had performed a deed of Camelotian proportion. One Holy Grail in a lifetime is more than we thought we'd ever get (certainly back in April '92), but to be granted a second?

With Keane replacing McClair and Kanchelskis eventually securing his right-wing berth, United provided the most expressive version of 'English' 4–4–2 there's ever been. Eighties Liverpool may have won more but did they ever excite as much as this? Eric, after years of searching, had found his true *métier*; from the moment of his return at The Dell in August, celebrated with the most divine of chipped goals, he revelled in his new position as the brain of the champions. After years of being treated as a mere adornment or even potential liability within a variety of incomplete, inconsistent sides, he could now enjoy applying the final brush-strokes to a masterpiece. For football's pre-eminent artist, what could be more fulfilling?

The memories of his most thrilling expositions should trip off the Red tongue: the derbies, Norwich, Villa and Oldham in December, Sheffield Wednesday in the snow, the epiphany at Wembley et cetera et cetera. But there was one special day for all of us when football had to take second place to a greater concern yet still look to itself to provide fitting tribute. Everton at home, 22 January: Sir Matt Busby's seat, alone in the packed stadium, empty; so too a season full of colourful joy, at one place paused for moments of black sorrow. Eric, a newcomer to our football world and only a recent addition to the United family, might have been excused for not fully appreciating what Matt's death – and, indeed, his life – meant to us. Amid the outpourings of emotion, one could have understood had Eric remained apart from it all. And it's all too easy at such times to string together the right clichés of commiseration for the sake of correctness. But unlike many players who look only for the next game or pay-packet, whose vision of football's horizons dims the further they look away from themselves, Eric has always displayed a feeling for and understanding of the spirit great men bring to both football and life. His discourse is peppered with the appreciation of legends, with illustrations of how the deeds of the giants have illuminated his own thoughts and touched his own sentiments. If you look at what Eric has said about Sir Matt, in particular about the example he gave us of 'kindness, courage, resilience and gentility', you cannot mistake the sincerity. And if you remember that he and his apprentice Giggs combined that day against Everton to demonstrate how Busby taught United the manner in which our football must be played, you will surely acknowledge that Eric has the right to include himself in his observation, 'you sense that Sir Matt's blood runs through every vein of the club's body'. By giving one of his most outstanding displays of the season that day, he paid his tribute in the best way he knew how, from one painter of masterpieces to another. (>> Julius Caesar)

Melissa Moore

Living proof that not all girlies watch footie for the butts 'n' thighs. Known to many Reds as 'the girl with the flag', she's such a committed Francophile that she penned this direct homage to send to Eric in her best A-level French. It can be no coincidence that the number of schoolies grappling with the 'subjonctif' and the oddness of 'être' has increased markedly since November 1992; an A-level examiner tells me Eric's the most popular subject in the oral examination.

Cantona. Puis-je tutoyer? Ton nom m'inspire de rappeler deux incidents imprimés sur mon cerveau. La première souvenir était le 6 février 1993, le trentecinquième anniversaire de la tragédie de Munich. Les équipes ont cerclé le milieu-terrain, la tête s'inclinant, en observant la minute de silence pour les Busby Babes. Ce jour-ci était la première introduction de l'histoire impressionante de Manchester United pour toi. Tu as bien compris la signification de la date. Quand la reste de l'équipe a semblé un peu opprimé par l'atmosphère lourd des souvenirs des pertes, toi, tu as pris ton role dirigeant actuel. Après avoir perdu un but par Franz Carr, nous nous sommes reveillés et le but egalisateur par Ryan Giggs était créé par toi-même. Mais les tribunes ont demandé plus. Là, au Stretford End modifié, j'ai crié du fond du coeur quand tu as reçu le ballon devant le goal. Le tir était spectaculaire, bouclant au coin du filet. Ta réaction: de sauter en célébration devant le Scoreboard Paddock et les fans orgasmiques. Tu as bien compris, tu étais l'un d'entre nous, soutenant la renommée du club et les joueurs de cinquante-huit.

L'autre fois était ton retour, le jour plus attendu que la deuxième arrivée de Jésus. Tous les pubs autour du stade étaient vides une heure avant le coup d'envoi quand tu as commencé ton échauffage. Les cris de la foule n'étaient que les chansons de toi, surtout *La Marseillaise*; les gradins ont vibré de 'Ooh-Ah' et 'We'eeeeell'. Ton premier passe a trouvé Nicky Butt qui a marqué le premier but. Classique Cantona. Les tricouleurs étaient sorties et Old Trafford était couvert de bleu, blanc et surtout rouge.

Mais notre euphorie n'a pas duré longtemps. Fowler a marqué deux buts et était sur le point de ruiner le grand jour de notre roi. Mais encore le destin est intervenu: l'arbitre a montré le point de reparation. Qui va le prendre? Nous l'avons su. Le tension était visible, tout le monde priait, même Kiddo et Fergie. Tu devais marquer, nous ne pouvions pas perdre, pas aujourd'hui. Et là, avec le col relévé, étais toi, d'un air nonchalant –

et le ballon. Et . . . BUT!!! 'Buteur numero sept – Eric Cantona.' Tu n'as rien perdu: la vision, le controle, tout toujours là. Notre virtuose nous a sauvé: le resultat ne fait rien à ce moment-là car tu as retrouvé ton equipe et nous as rendus contents.

Je voudrais profiter de l'occasion pour te remercier, Monsieur Cantona, pour tous les buts, passes et matches où on a vu ton génie et aussi pour le fait que tu nous comprends. Nous, la bande de supporters qui chantons *La Marseillaise* plus que notre propre hymne national, les Francophiles de Manchester, et tous les autres lieux rouges. Merci Eric, le vrai successeur de Roi Denis. Vive le roi du maillot rouge, toujours dans nos coeurs au théâtre des rêves.

Merchandise

A word usually spat out with contempt; nothing summons up the spirit of the plc, commercialism, naff exploitation and day-tripper domination like it. Club merchandise used to mean three varieties of scarf, some pennants and a couple of badges sold from a glorified hut. Now under the roof of the Temple of the Tasteless that is the United Megastore, Cantona and every other player is simply a form of colouring on every conceivable item you would use – and plenty you wouldn't. (A 'Fred The Red' desk-tidy anyone?)

Yet even amongst this tawdry, gaudy collection of tat, those with the Cantona imprimatur stand out. The Number Seven shirt is, of course, a classic: nobody can quibble there. But what would otherwise be tacky rubbish is transformed because it is Cantonesque. I confess here to owning two official Cantona T-shirts. Why is it that a T-shirt with, say, Roy Keane's picture on it is awful while Eric's print is acceptable? After all, Keano is virtually a god himself. It is surely because the pictorial image of Eric has been transformed. It is no longer a mere likeness or representation but an icon in itself. Any plain shirt featuring any Eric picture – virtually no uncool Eric pics exist – is an instant artefact for iconographers everywhere.

Well, that's my defence anyway. The truly collectable stuff is outside on the barrows and stalls where the street artists ply their wares. The story of Eric at United could be told visually just by assembling the endless variety of Eric-worshipping shirts in chronological order. While the official designers lumber on six months behind the times, the Warwick Road boys offer an up-to-the-minute cultural commentary. Along with the fanzines, this is the tangible evidence of contemporary terrace opinion. Within three weeks of Eric's arrival, there were seven Cantona varieties out on display, the surest sign to date that the man was a hit. Within three days of Selhurst Park you could choose from a comprehensive range of pro-Eric declarations mounted on cotton. The turnover is phenomenal; in a sense, they are pure expressions of pop art – instant, in your face, disposable yet sometimes enduring. (The classic L'Eric Sportif is much missed.) And as long as their creativity is maintained, they will never be defeated by the would-be monopolists inside Old Trafford.

It was often proposed by cynics during 1995 that

United would never sell Eric because they couldn't handle the consequent merchandising loss. Bollocks, of course: the merchandising operation profit is nowhere near as great as myth would have it. Nevertheless, it has been suggested that during the Cantona contract talks an attempt was made to secure a large percentage of all Eric-related merchandise profit for the player himself. For the time being, this concept has been stamped upon as it would set a dangerous precedent. But as player-power increases – and this has been made explicit by several stars – individual players will take back the rights to their own images and be in a position to demand the bulk of any proceeds. Good: when the players become solely responsible for their own gear, the taste level will improve immeasurably. I can't see Eric sanctioning Cantona bog-roll, can you?

'N' is for . . .

NFFSC

The National Federation of Football Supporters' Clubs is, along with the Football Supporters' Association, one of the two bodies to whom the media will go for a 'fans'-eye' quote; both are jostling for pre-eminent position as the Labour Party dangles the promise of a seat at the top table in the event of a Blair government. I know of many fans who've had cause to be grateful for the FSA's practical help and support in the past but I've yet to meet anyone who can say the same for the NFFSC. Indeed, as far as Reds are concerned, the all too frequent sight of the unlovely Ms Hartland on our screens has caused many a turned stomach; the fact that their publicity material has been used approvingly to back the loathsome 'anti-prole' agenda of some in charge at Old Trafford hasn't endeared them to us either. Of the near-200 United supporters clubs, only three are affiliated to them; perhaps that explains why they felt safe enough to go public with a call to ban Eric from our game for good.

Whilst the FSA and their admirable Palace fan chairman Tim Crabbe played a straight and fair bat, Tony

Kershaw put out a press release that oozed both sen-
sationalism and moral cowardice; essentially, they said
Eric had to go because his presence at games would
incite violence. So much for the philosophy we are all
supposed to share that we don't cave in to intimidation
and mob-law. Now that their blood-curdling predictions
have signally failed to materialize, their silence is deafening and damning. When the battle comes that decides
who will speak for us all, don't let that squalid episode
slip your mind.

Admittedly, there was a point when bodies like the
NFFSC could have claimed a popular mandate for their
anti-Eric policy. For the first few days, 90 per cent of
other clubs' fans were gleefully running with the mob,
chucking half-bricks at us and generally enjoying the
open goal we'd presented them. Who could blame them?
Don't tell me that your first instinct, had the miscreant
been Shearer or Fowler, wouldn't have been to let rip a
rampantly subjective howl of 'String 'em up!' No true
fan can even try to be objective in the heat of such a
moment. When an opponent goes down, you follow in
with both boots – those fans were just doing their duty.
Reds seemed to appreciate that too; their enemies were
the media and authorities, not other fans.

Once subjective passion was spent, dispassionate
analysis had its day. Within the month, and certainly
after the court case, other fans had apparently reassessed
their opinions. Polls shifted towards a fifty-fifty split over
whether Eric should be allowed to return. For some, a
greater love for the art of football had overcome their
ABU sentiment; others fell into line behind the anti-

racist campaign; many appeared simply to have realized that life would be far more entertaining with Eric around, especially if he had another funny turn. Of course there is still hostility and hatred – Eric still remains the personification of the United spirit and is therefore a primary target – but much of the crowd abuse he has received since his comeback has been half-hearted and ritualistic, a tactic for the first twenty minutes that becomes tedious. There will always be the sporadic death threats and 'incidents' but then there always had been before '95. The truth, perhaps, is that Radio Five's two Dannys had it right when they reckoned that most fans just found the kung-fu funny: the outrage was opportunistic rather than principled. And after all, within every ostensible Cantona-hater's heart there lurks the deepest truth: they all wished he played for them.

Nimes

A beautiful town and a cute club: cruel, then, that this should have been the final hellish inferno that consumed any remaining Cantona desire for French football. But there was Purgatory before Hell, of course: the old devil Tapie still had one more season of prodding Eric with his bent, corrupted trident at OM before Eric left for good.

Back from Montpellier by popular demand, the despoiled shirt apparently forgiven, Eric could look forward to a regime he could handle – Beckenbauer in charge, Tapie keeping his fat meddlesome digits to himself and his brown envelopes. With Waddle and Papin

providing proper support at last, Eric scored seven in his
first 12 games back as OM raced to the top of the table.
After that aborted first run, Eric was finally taking off.
Then disaster struck. On 28 October 1990 a Brest trun-
dler hacked Eric from behind, detaching ligaments.
Recovery took three months. When you realize that this
cost Eric his dream of emulating boyhood heroes, perhaps it can be appreciated why he has since reacted so
badly to the sinister attentions of England's hatchetmen,
untrammelled by officials' 'protection'.

When Eric returned, Beckenbauer had been shunted
aside, Tapie manoeuvring as of old to bring in the loathsome Goethals. Belgians and Frenchmen have strained
relationships in general anyway, but this mismatch was
personal too. Just because Eric can be a bit paranoid
doesn't mean they're not out to get him, however; club
insiders were already spreading news that Eric's death
warrant had been signed. As Eric, understandably,
struggled to get fully sharpened, his first team appearances were restricted to half a dozen. And when Eric
refused to back Tapie against the authorities after the
wideboy opened his mouth too far *vis-à-vis* the parent-
hood of a referee, the grim dénouement was inevitable.
Eric got the championship medal he deserved, for his
eight goals had been invaluable, but Tapie got the scalp
he'd sought. As Eric pointed out wryly, Goethals may
well have taken the public 'credit' but he knew who'd
been pulling the strings. For Tapie, who had tried to
build himself into a hideous conglomeration of Mayor
Daley, Jack Walker and Silvio Berlusconi, there was
clearly only room for one self-possessed, wilful colossus

at OM. How Eric must have enjoyed the sight of the mogul's later downfall.

Sold to Nimes half-price, Eric eked out the saddest of codas to his French career. Captain of a side without style or great ambition, he endured six increasingly miserable months of 1991/2 battling with his own dispirited lack of form and a hostile public. Two goals in eighteen games told its own story. Nimes was simply not a Cantonesque side; the final conflagration in December was surely a merciful release for club and player. Following his memorable confrontation with Jacques Riolaci's stuffed shirts (>> Authority), he announced on 12 December 1991 that he was retiring from football. If Eric has been France's George Best, then quitting at twenty-five outdid even Georgie's premature farewell. If only Best had had a Platini or a Houllier on hand to rescue him . . . fortunately for us all, Eric did. (>> Elba)

Norwich

Looking back from 1996, it now seems ridiculously quaint that titanic championship battles could ever have taken place at Carrow Road. The mystery of Norwich's rise is only further wrapped up in enigma when you consider how Messrs Walker and Chase have performed since. It never seemed real did it? Somehow you always knew they'd all be much happier getting back to tractor-fondling and shagging grow-bags.

Strangely enough, Norwich crops up regularly in any litany of Cantona highlights: his first full game, of course; his first serious brush with domestic aggro in '94's Cup tie; and two of his greatest exhibitions of showmanship in the home League games of '94 and '95. Perhaps the fact that Norwich were always into the passing game, clean and easily intimidated, brought out both the godly and devilish in Eric. But the greatest of all East Anglian assignments took place on the night of 5 April 1993.

It had been almost a fortnight since our last game, a stereotypically dull 0-0 with the Gooners, a fortnight full of innuendo and ill wishful thinking from the ABU brigade. We were 'on the wobble', without a win in five, possibly heading for yet another Easter cross to bear. Eric, though, had maintained his consistency, saving us at Maine Road; he was now firmly established as the team's linchpin. At crossroads such as these, great men define themselves. With both Villa and Norwich threatening to make the break from us, Ferguson seized the moment: eschewing his old ways of safety-first, he chose all-out attack. If football, like politics, is the art of the possible, then Cantona's gift to us all has been to inspire those around him to raise their horizons and make what was improbable seem possible. He took up the manager's challenge and orchestrated one of the most viscerally thrilling displays we'd seen.

The bare facts – three goals in eight minutes, the first made by Eric, the third finished – are all that the history books will record. Mention may be made of the myriad chances that found woodwork or Gunn's desperate clutches. But you had to be there to understand how wondrous it was to watch a sorcerer and his apprentices play football of the purest brilliance. Not only that, it was the context of it: you just don't expect to see teams under so much pressure in such an important match play with this daring exuberance. And though the Wayne's World genuflections were for Robbo when he came on, the time had almost come for the crown to be passed on; the era of 'Eric The King' was upon us. At the beginning, he had been regarded as a 'mere' catalyst in this champion reaction: surely now he was virtually a core element. The ten-out-of-ten marks were scattered freely for Eric next day – United as a team scarcely looked back from then on in. Rightly, one of the BC old guard, Stevie Bruce, had his moment under the laurels the following week but as the statistics show, and as your feelings tell you – this glittering Premiership crown came courtesy of much French polish. (>> City)

'O' is for . . .

October Revolution

. . . as the T-shirts dubbed Eric's comeback; 'Red October'
or 'The Return Of The Magnificent Seven' were popular
alternatives. Steve Black, trusted lieutenant of United We
Stand and the travelling Red Army, dons his Henri Lloyd
thinking cap and reflects upon resurrection.

With poise and grace, the man who would be King had
come to Britain, exiled from his native land – Eric le
Dauphin, made to wait for his birthright. *Mais non*. His
true homeland beckoned within foreign shores as the
lost people asked him to lead us out of the wilderness
that had been twenty-six years. But he was to be banished
again. We would wait. Could he? Of course. October
the First . . .

So we sang Hosannah to the King of Kings. A lover
returns home after a nine-month trip abroad. Could it
be the same? Would it? Please let it. Hindu statues
drinking milk? No coincidence surely. The Messiah
returning. Blasphemy? No. Eric's no false idol. We had
drunk from the Holy Grail only after his crusades
had brought him to his spiritual home. Our home. The

pain of Munich. The pleasure of Best, Law and Charlton. The legend of Busby. There was no other place. Avalon – Old Trafford. Mancunian men voting Cantona as the person most wanted to holiday with said more than the thousands of words in the media one week BC. Nothing to forgive. Nothing to forget. An indiscretion any of us would have committed. Outrageous punishment: crucifixion. Unsurprisingly, he rose again. Two minutes into the new – the ball at his feet. The world at his feet. A cross. A goal. Simple. Beautiful. Nineteen minutes to go, defeat looming – the ball at his feet. A pass. A penalty. A goal. Of course a goal. Thank you.

So that was it. Nothing to worry about. A return to the soil that had created a legend, paradoxically the most blindly adored yet viciously hated man in football. But it would have been wrong for him to have played for any other team than ours, the only team to evoke precisely the same polarity of emotions. Nobody could ever have replaced Robson in the Number Seven shirt yet there was our very own Messiah making it his own. Leading from the front, taking up arms (and legs) when necessary to defend the rights of himself and all that is good and Red. Eric the philosopher, poet, artist and *artiste*. Defender of the Faith. Eric the footballer: the best of all time.

Olympique Marseilles

When Eric came on to the market in the summer of '88, every desperate Cinderella and sleeping giant in French football saw in him exactly what Ferguson did over four years later – a genuine Great White Hope, the sort of catalysing personality who could lift an entire club, a purgative tonic for players and fans alike. Within weeks, only two rivals were left at the poker table with the sufficient resources – twenty-two million francs and a 1,000 per cent salary hike – to tempt both Auxerre and Cantona: Olympique Marseilles and Matra Racing of Paris. For Eric, this should have been the career-defining moment of choice, and in a way it was, though hardly with the consequences of which Eric was then dreaming.

Racing Club of Paris, without a trophy since 1949 and now well under the heel of St Germain's trendy Left Bank boots, were attempting a Parma-style revival under the aegis of arms merchants Matra. They offered Eric much that would otherwise have been irresistible: the cultural feast of Paris, the partnership of the graceful Francescoli and the personal sponsorship of club president Lagardère, always a useful security amidst the standard Euro-club politicking. It is not known whether the president knew of the younger Eric's choice of Auxerre over Nice being brokered by a free club shirt; whatever, he was astute enough to recognize Eric's appreciation of these symbols and gestures. Sweet-talking Cantona over dinner, an original Miro hanging seductively over the mantelpiece, the Matra boss proffered exquisitely produced coffee-table tomes about both Miro and Picasso; Eric was as impressed as John Lennon had been when Allen Klein recited 'Nowhere Man' to him and thus won the Beatles' managerial contract. Had Matra's bid-war opponents been anyone but OM, that instinct of the fourteen-year-old Cantona would surely have taken him north. But within hours of this meeting, Eric had chosen Marseilles. They were, after all, 'his club'. It seems that even if Matra's profits of death had run to an Ambrogiani original, the Caillols boy would not have been deflected.

Most accounts of his first turbulent spell at the Stade Vélodrome go something like this. Within weeks, a case of the blundering Birtles is diagnosed – he fails to score in his opening five games. Distracted by the imbroglio with Henri Michel (>> Authority), some fans think he's dwelling, Sharpe-style, on his international problems rather than those of his wage-paying club. As the crowd grows impatient, he collapses under the pressure: five goals in his opening twenty-two games is not what you expect for twenty-two million francs. When the final confrontation comes, everyone at OM is glad to see the back of him as Tapie packs him off to the Girondins.

Naturally, the truth is rather more shaded. Talking to some of the fans who were there, one discovers that they were split over Eric. The 'Cantonistas' faction gave him a bedrock of unyielding support, founded on their love of a true southern spirit battling against the odds to resurrect the club he supported from the terraces. His fiercest critics, by contrast, often appeared to be the newer arrivals who'd come to the Vélodrome in the previous two years to join the Tapie bandwagon. United fans will appreciate the scenario more than most.

As for his actual form, admittedly the ten out of ten marks from *FranceFoot* were in short supply. But then, in the OM team he was hardly the only one in such a trough. Eric began to feel singled out, a scapegoat for

a larger failure left to swing from the tree amid a whirlwind of media criticism. As the big signing, he knew
that would be his fate; what he might have expected was
a little more support from those within the club. He also
talked of his sense of disorientation, complaining that he
didn't know what was expected of him; suggestions of
tactical misunderstandings and a lack of direction from
the top appeared to be verified by the dull sludginess
of the player and team. There was something else too, a
sense that by stepping back into his old world he had
lost an edge. At the time, there was no defeatism. Even
at the moment of crisis, *they* expelled *him*; he didn't run
away. But later, he wondered aloud about the wisdom
of exchanging his erstwhile existentialist route of voyage,
change and challenge for a return to home, comfort and
belonging: 'Going back put me in the past – I slipped
back ten years to my amateur days.' More prosaically, he
also saw that he was still a touch too young to take up
a whole club's burden and struggle with it in front of
such an audience every week.

In January 1989, Eric joined OM for a charity match
against Torpedo. The venue was Sedan, scene of disgrace
and defeat in 1870 for another French emperor who
split his legions, Napoleon the Third. Provoked by crowd
jeering, but symptomatic of a deeper malaise, Eric
booted the ball into the stands, threw his shirt towards
the ref in disgust and stalked off to be substituted. Within
two weeks, after escaping the media hounds in a Barce-
lonian *séjour*, he had been indefinitely suspended by
Tapie and sent on loan to Bordeaux. It was archetypal
Cantona: a rush of instinct, a *grand geste* and a physical

expression of a spiritual sickness. Rather than looking for the explanations of such a *cri de coeur*, the media simply whipped him into the stocks for a public flaying. For a while, he lost the support of all but the Cantonistas in the Stade, the white OM shirt being regarded by fans as reverentially as the tricolour itself. Eric stayed stoically true to his own moral code in the face of the onslaught, accepting full responsibility, explaining that he needed to tell the public they were being cheated but regretting only the media image created by the incident, not the actual incident and meaning itself. For now he was an outcast, the outsider on a voyage once more: he would return to take on Tapie and restore the Marseillaises' faith in him when he was good and ready. (>> Stade de Mosson)

'P' is for . . .

Platini

If Eric is the George Best of French football, then Michel Platini is the Bobby Charlton, a nation's favourite son and incarnation of its nobler values. Thankfully, the analogy doesn't extend much further. Whilst Bobby and George have always struggled to conceal their mutual antagonism, Cantona and Platini have forged not only a relationship of mentor and student but also a genuine friendship. It is telling that despite the deep personal disappointment Eric felt over France's Euro '92 disaster, his first thought was for departing manager Platini: 'He is the one for whom I will always have an eternal respect and admiration . . . we would all have wished, so loved was he, that he had left with the victory he merited. I would even have played in goal if he'd asked me!' Five months earlier, it had been Platini who'd burned telephone lines hot then inveigled managers and agents to rescue Eric from his post-Nimes exile, placing his own reputation on the line by vouching for Eric and being the man we must all credit for saving this talent for their nation and our club.

Apologies to songsmith Peter Boyle for contradicting

his lyric '[Eric's] the greatest French footballer that the world has ever seen', but as Cantona would be the first to concede, that accolade is Platini's. There are parallels in their respective careers: Platini was also very much the provincial, born in Jouef and never a big city star in France; he too hit the most exalted heights abroad, at Juventus; and his game was also reliant on vision and brain rather than pace or power. There are so many Platinian facets in Eric's play that it is obvious he devoted as much time to studying Michel as he did Johann or Franz; that identical pre-touch reconnaissance for which they both raise their heads is typical testament to lessons passed on from Platini's trainer father to son and then on to Eric.

Of course any French player must hold up Platini as an example; it's as *de rigueur* as a British pop group paying homage to the Beatles. But there is a case to be made that the idolatry is particularly relevant to Eric. Despite his devil-may-care attitude, he is on record as expressing a desire to be properly appreciated by all who see him – not just Reds and confirmed Cantonistas but by all who profess to love football. Platini won just such admiration. Even when his St Etienne side were putting all to the sword, Platini remained immensely popular with all French fans; his success abroad was greeted with pride by those not used to seeing triumphant French sporting exports. Moreover, the goals that Platini achieved are precisely those that Eric has admitted he has yet to fulfil – European victory and international pre-eminence. Those life-defining moments that secure world acclaim came to Platini. His pass led to a European

Cup winning penalty which he converted; his winner in that unbelievable Euro '84 semi-final – greeted by the most frenzied roar John Motson has ever let rip – sealed his position as a national hero. These are the kind of moments Eric still yearns for; no one will be more delighted than his friend Michel should he achieve them.

Pride

. . . yes, yes, 'goes before a fall': so what? Better to walk tall and occasionally fall on your arse than scuttle through life bent double under the weight of modesty. Eric can seem arrogant but then he has much to be arrogant about; he can occasionally appear pompous, but then few great and proud men can escape that accusation. Fortunately, most who know him speak of his pride as a positive characteristic, as an unavoidable product of a natural nobility ('He is an island of pride and generosity,' purrs Houllier). Moreover, the French in general do not yet suffer from the post-imperial self-loathing of the Brits. Those who have got the best from Eric during his career are those who have understood this essential Cantona facet. Fergie plays up to it superbly as did Platini; conversely, those who ignore it pay the price. When Trevor Francis asked Eric to trial for an extra week, Cantona's response was hugely predictable: proud actors do not 'audition' alongside amateurs.

Still, football is full of 'egomaniacs' who bristle at the merest perception of slight; there are plenty of canny operators about who have sufficiently honed their man-management skills to be able to handle them. But even the most hardened of proud English pros can be prepared to step forward and say sorry, or promise to change their attitudes, when nemesis follows hubris; they might not necessarily mean it but see it as politic. Not Eric. That there was no public apology following Selhurst Park and no *mea culpa* PR spread in the tabloids was typical Cantona. Many French observers have noted, often with approval, that he is simply too proud to give regretful explanations. Instead he assumes responsibility for his actions and takes whatever comes silently like an existential hero. Did Cantona's demeanour during 1995 not recall that of Mersault in *The Outsider*? Many assume that Eric's pride still conceals a fundamental regret. But is that regret – he was reported by Fergie to be 'devastated' the next day – more for the consequences and the harm done to friends than for the act itself? Many who spoke to Eric in the aftermath said he felt that he had done nothing morally wrong; the damage had been to his image, not his soul.

Two Cantona quotes help lead us towards an explanation: 'He who has regrets grimaces in the mirror when he wakes. He is a traitor to others – and above all he is betraying himself.' And: 'Whatever people say, no one will make me change; I'll only change when I want to.' Firstly, Eric believes in acting upon instinct. Why? Because that is how you act true to yourself. How can you regret an action that is true and honest in your own judgement? To apologize for yourself is either to lie or to admit that your action was not true to yourself in the first place. That kick, for example, was no aberration – in its execution, dramatic style and cause, it was purest

Cantona. To apologize for it would be to apologize for one's very existence. Secondly, like Mersault, Eric knows that change to fit the morality of others is both inexcusable and impossible; one's own morality is one's only 'god'. Sorry seems to be the hardest word for good reason.

Provincialism

If you think London and the provinces have a problematic relationship, you should hear what the Parisians and the rest say about each other in France: historian academics call it the 'centre-periphery disparity'. Throughout history Paris and the regions have often appeared to develop like separate countries – Israel and Iran spring to mind – and there are no Parisophobes as avid as the Marseillaises. Imagine the anti-London sentiments of Manchester, Liverpool and Newcastle combined in one concentration – that would be the equivalent of Eric's home city. He has never needed our particular North–South divide explained to him because he comes from an area where people talk of the 'Parisian colonists' and plot regional liberationism. The French metropolitan sophisticates can sneer at Eric for being so typically 'provincial', they may laugh at his southern accent and they might disparage his adherence to traditional regional culture, but any proud Mancunian welcomes such attitudes. You could say that the road from Manchester to Marseilles is really much shorter than the one to London. Parisians, especially those who support Paris St Germain, are just about the only French who'll favour David Ginola over Cantona. As Eric is an ex-Olympique Marseilles player, that would be inevitable anyway; the relationship between PSG and OM is as hostile as that between United and Liverpool but bears the added, loaded value of the eternal conflict between city and province. Outside Paris, Cantona gains the support of every Frenchman who welcomes the anti-metropolis and anti-establishment figure. This perhaps explains why press and public opinion about Eric is so out-of-kilter: 90 per cent of the sports punditocracy live inside the Paris *periphèrique*, 90 per cent of the people outside.

Eric's footballing triumphs in France were at the expense of Parisians – his Montpellier outsiders robbing Racing Club in the Cup, his OM team beating off St Germain for the title – but it has been his latter-day stance that has marked him out as a bolshie provincial. He laid into capital golden boy Ginola for costing France a World Cup place, then argued that international matches should be taken away from Paris and given to the provinces. Declaring that the support of 45,000 at the Parc des Princes was inferior in quality to that which 30,000 could provide at St Etienne didn't endear him to Parisians; his frequent attacks on the football media cultural élite have rightly been seen as coded digs at the capital's charmed circles. Indeed, whenever Eric makes criticisms of the French way of doing things, he seems to use the adjective 'French' when in fact 'Parisian' would've been more accurate. As in England, where middle-class south-eastern values have become seen by outsiders as quintessentially representative of the whole of England, France's image has been hijacked by Paris. (Go to the south, then see if you recognize the stereotype of the French as snooty, rude and pretentious.) To the metropolitan, Eric's provincialist pride may make him even more of an outsider, but to a Mancunian, he becomes even more 'one of us'.

'Q' is for . . .

Quietism

A form of religious mysticism which my dictionary defines as 'A passive attitude towards life with devotional contemplation and abandonment of the will on non-resistance principles'. As I write in March 1996, those same hacks who once lambasted Eric as irredeemably violent now talk of 'Saint Eric' – he has apparently undergone a Damascene conversion to quietism. Those fantastically unhinged attempts at tackling back are now consigned to distant memory. It's as if Eric's a lofty godfather who delegates dirty matters to his underlings, leaving them to exact retaliation for patent injustices. Errant referees provoke quizzical raised eyebrows instead of hurled mitres. And when it's time for a team bundle, Eric plays the peacemaker, floating into the fray to separate combatants and give Cole a sly cuff.

There was a point, around Christmas 1995, when some Reds wondered out loud whether this new version of Eric was wholly welcome. Hadn't he always talked of his necessary fire and passion which, although it may occasionally do harm, made him the star performer that he is? If that blaze had been reduced to a mere smoulder, then wouldn't he in turn become a less effective player? Certainly for a while he seemed less involved, less committed, even – dare one say it – a touch afraid. Glad though we were to see a reduction in the number of his indictable offences, there was still something sad about the epitome of fearlessness being cowed by the threat of Damoclean sword.

Perhaps it was all just a matter of getting the right balance between passion and prudence for, since the turn of the year, he has come back to his best. It's as if he has now worked out precisely how to synthesize all the differing and often contradictory demands placed upon him by manager, press, authorities and fans into one *modus operandi* acceptable to all. The sole Cantona facet that is predictable is his very unpredictability, so only a fool would bet his season ticket on Eric never succumbing to the red mists again. But so far the prognosis is encouraging: in the lingo of the probationer, he appears to have addressed his reoffending behaviour and secured his continuing parole.

Whether Eric is actually a changed man is an entirely different question. We know how central instinctiveness is to him: is it that the instinct to strike back still lurks but is overpowered by the primary instinct of self-preservation? In terms of the struggle between essentialism and existentialism, is the nature of Eric's character still unchanged but his impulse to action altered by a strict, self-imposed new moral code? Never underestimate the exis power of reinvention. Or is it a function of the separation of image (>>) and reality that has so often worked against him but which for once he is manipulating in his favour? Admittedly exile, like prison, can fundamentally change the values of even so strong-willed and principled a man as Eric. But the suspicion must be that the real challenge is still to come, and that if it does, it will reveal Eric is a long way from being ready to join the Tibetan quietists just yet.

One young Red we thought was a bit of a quietist is Jamie Smith, who joined the K-Standers both for their recording sessions and the expeditionary force sent down to Croydon Magistrates. Post-verdict, however, he exploded with rage into several TV cameras and apparently led news bulletins across Europe with his damning denunciations of the media and judiciary. Here he reflects upon the Messiah with some apt religious imagery.

While it's well known that no player can be bigger than the club, surely Eric (as with Elvis, Marilyn and Jesus, the first name suffices) has come closer than most to achieving this impossible feat. After all, Law, Best and Charlton were more often referred to as part of a Holy Trinity rather than as individual superstars; Robson, as captain of England, was universally admired but Eric, he's all ours and ours alone.

Whether he's churning out contenders for goal of the month, spitting on bestial cretins, charming everyone at the PFA Awards or simply leaving incompetent defenders on their backsides, everything Eric does is in the United style: 'I've got class and don't mind showing it – if you don't like it, f*ck off.' From his upturned collars to the adopted Manc swagger, it's easy to understand why the adage was coined: 'He wasn't born Red but he was born to be Red.'

This one's more than a footballer. He's a poet, an artist, a model, a writer, a movie star and even a vigilante with his infamous 'blow for freedom' last year. The gutter press howled, treating him with the disdain reserved for child-killers and the like. Funny how the editorial stance of these rags is that drug pushers, rapists and joy-riders should be castrated and 'have-a-go heroes' given gold stars, yet someone who gives a racist thug a good dig is persecuted. Eric does seem to have something in common with Jesus Christ. Ridiculed and resented by the ignorant rabble who fail to appreciate his talent for making the miraculous happen, but revered by those in the know. Eric has considerably more than twelve disciples, although his own particular resurrection took nine months rather than the standard three days.

Since his Second Coming, Eric's passionate fire has burned with the discipline of a Bunsen burner rather than the raging inferno of old. Some might say this has reduced him as a player but Eric is now back to his best, only without the problems with referees. Since 1991, every time he's finished the season he has done so as a champion. Should the Reds prove successful, it would be a big two-fingered salute to everyone who wanted to send him packing last January.

And with his new-found temperament, who better to take the reins when Fergie steps down in a few years time? Unlikely? Stranger things have happened. As an overweight Cockney pisshead once said, it is a funny old game.

Quislings

For the most part, the range of public commentators who made up the post-Selhurst Cantona firing squad was tiresomely predictable, from the unctuous sanctimony of Lineker to the hypocrisy of Alan Mullery, once disgraced as England's first sending-off. Never was the difference between tabloid and broadsheet more evident too: as the tabloids strove to outdo each other in ferocity of condemnation, the qualities played host to the more intelligent reflections of Peter Corrigan, Jim White *et al*. The grudging disappointment displayed by the tabloid rats when Eric re-signed said everything about their motivation: they no longer seek the news as such, just victims to string up. What one might have hoped for is that United men stayed true to the colours; sadly some chose the Norwegian option.

TOMMY DOCHERTY
As ever, first on the scene with a rent-a-quote. Perhaps he was simply following his usual policy of saying the opposite of whatever Paddy Crerand believes; it was a final disillusionment for many Red Army vets. Compounded his naughtiness by appearing to back Eric when live on TV, surrounded by handy Reds, before going back to his old 'kick him out' line when in the safety of a studio.

ALEX STEPNEY
The first ex-player to shriek that Eric should be banned for life and sacked. Unforgivably invoked the authority

of one who can no longer say his own piece – Matt Busby. A tasteless device and one that Mr Crerand had no truck with; after all, if we're playing 'who knew Matt best?' games, Stepney's occasional golf rounds hardly compete with Pat's unique Busby relationship.

GARTH CROOKS

Ex-Red, though you'd never guess so. Hit Lineker levels of sanctimony when appearing every hour on Sky – good appearance fees, Garth? Unlike John Barnes, Crooks's experience as a black player only made him less sympathetic to Eric's position, somewhat bizarrely.

JOHNNY GILES

Not a trace of sympathy for a man who's brought success to both Giles's major clubs. As Giles himself was once a byword for the combination of supreme skill and sly nastiness which he now accused Eric of representing, you could be forgiven for using the word hypocrite. Is this a good time to mention an early sixties court appearance featuring Giles and other United players for public misbehaviour involving attacks on passers-by in Urmston?

WILLIE MORGAN

In the classic 'Bert' cartoons, he's always drawn in a shirt bearing the legend 'Better Than Best'; here, he outdid his rival in condemnation of Eric – at least Best retracted his initial hostile comments. Port Vale away might go down as the last time we heard 'Willie Morgan On The Wing'.

LEN LAVELLE, SEAN S. MURRAY, STEPH
EDWARDS, CRAIG LOFTUS etc.
All 'Reds' who volunteered quotes to the press con-
demning Eric and demanding he be shown the door;
Lavelle even argues two weeks' prison wasn't enough.
Did they remain in their seats as Eric's 1995/6 goals
drove home? Compounded their *lèse-majesté* by mainly
doing so in News International scum-rags.

'R' is for . . .

The Rebel

Arguably the philosopher/goalie Albert Camus's greatest piece of non-fiction, an examination and barely concealed celebration of the philosophy of rebellion. French schoolies who've innocently enjoyed *The Outsider* and *The Plague* may find themselves cajoled by teachers into reading this next; before they know it, they're banged up in uni with Derrida groupies before spending a lifetime spouting bollocks on interminable 'Antenne 2' egghead shows. But for the ordinary Frenchman, the spirit of rebellion is instinctive, not instructed. This is a nation which, when particularly fed up with government in general, burns down the entire edifice and starts again at fifty-year intervals: revolution is chic – evolution is, well, just a bit too *style Anglais*. Our cultural icons – the Trollopes, Burkes and even Orwells – are still cosy and comforting; France's are spiky, disconcerting and dangerous. Indeed, our history could be interpreted as a constant battle to keep these Gallic viruses confined to the Continent; the fear and loathing that Cantona's arrival inspired in some has a good traditional grounding.

The natural rebelliousness of Eric's French spirit is exacerbated by his personal genetic and environmental inheritance. Ferocious Catalan and Sardinian bloodlines mix at the family's location, the turbulent, anti-capital and anti-capitalist Midi Rouge; add his own self-possessed individualism and spontaneous nature and it is hardly surprising that the code of the rebel dominates his morality. Look again at his heroes like Jim Morrison, Leo Ferre, Brando and Rimbaud – all outsiders and rebels, sometimes to self-destructive extent. Cantona may well now be a socialist but it is not too fanciful to suggest that had he been of his grandfather's generation, he would have been at home with the POUM anarchist brigades in Barca of whom Orwell wrote so admiringly in *Homage To Catalonia*. In modern Britain, sadly, the spirit, desirability and downright cool of the rebel died with the miners' hopes in 1984. In the dull, conformist world of Blair and Major, this facet of Cantona's nature – like so many other elements of his make-up – seems only quaint and old-fashioned to his detractors. Not so, of course, to the Cantonistas, striving to keep old flames burning.

He has at least been a rebel with a cause. There's been the unending struggle against what he sees as illegitimate, corrupt and unjust authority; the constant fight to secure freedom and self-expression in a profession that demands conformity and servility; the refusal to sacrifice his self-respect just in order 'to please others'. Such stands make life more difficult for both himself and those around him but then the suffering of the rebel was always a greater theme in the literature of rebellion.

I recall an article by Patrick Barclay in which he appeared to chastise Eric for 'choosing' personal icons who were so dangerously rebellious; he suggested that in attempting to emulate Rimbaud, Morrison or James Dean, Cantona risked similar early burn-out and personal disaster. Some people just don't get it do they? One does not really choose one's own icons; they are already there awaiting discovery. Eric didn't go along to see *Waterfront* and then think to himself, 'Ooh-la-la, I think I'll change my personality and become a Brando clone.' He has merely recognized and appreciated in others what he had already realized in himself. More importantly, so what if he burns out or loses everything in some trauma resulting from his reckless rebellion? All those historical figures who have done so have also gained immortality; would Rimbaud now inspire such devotion if he'd dribbled away into an increasingly conformist old age? Of course not: and surely his art would have suffered from that very process too. Eric, in an almost conscious nod to the *Rebel Without A Cause* himself, has said: 'A young man has a right to rebel. I have no time for longevity. Living fast and hard, that's what interests me.' (Though we hope this doesn't include emulating that rebel's late-night Porsche races.)

Cantona doesn't believe in life after death. All he has to concern himself with, apart from his family, is his historical legacy. And despite the current cultural climate of conformity, it is still and always will be the legend of the rebel that resonates the loudest across the subsequent generations. Long after the Keegans and Linekers have become mere statistics in record books, visions of the Bests and Cantonas will remain.

Red Issue

*T*he best-selling fanzine and arguably the focus for the *heartland of Cantona's support; in the kung-fu wake, for example, this was not the place to look for expressions of contrition. Typical was Monsieur Légume in his immediate verdict: 'He is the King – he can do no wrong.' Here he tells of a symbolic Cantona moment from the other side of the world that suggests Sir Bobby's iconic status is under threat.*

Serving my football supporting apprenticeship in that barren period some ten years after United had won the European Cup, I was always aware of tales told of the fame which that side had attained and how the very words 'Bobby Charlton' had become a soccer Esperanto abroad for those Reds whose linguistic capabilities did not stretch beyond *biera*. Little did I realize that many years later the name 'Cantona' would act as a similar catalyst.

I had been travelling on the Malaysian east coast in the summer of 1995 and was waiting at Kota Baru bus station to go to Kuala Lumpur, twelve hours' ride away, to watch United in one of the most meaningless of the many such Red friendlies I've seen in recent years. I'd already been waiting two hours or so when three boys, two no more than nine or ten, began to sell burgers and corn cobs from a small stall. I can't resist food and by this time was starving so, no matter how unhygienic the cooking facilities were, I had to have my burger. Kota Baru would hardly qualify as a tourist hotspot and we were the only Europeans in the station so when I approached the young lads, I had hoped that by pointing and with a bit of luck I might get my order across to them. I needn't have worried. The thirteen-year-old asked, 'Hey mister, where you from?' 'England,' I replied. 'Where in England?' 'Manchester.' 'Ah, Manchester, Manchester United – Eric Cantona!' As he spoke our immortal Gallic hero's name, he took three or four steps back from his stall and proceeded to do his best Power Rangers kung-fu kick, mimicking the Frenchman's at Selhurst the previous January.

Once it became clear that I was a Red, he left his younger brothers to look after the stall whilst we talked football, United and Cantona. I learned that in a recent Malaysian Second Division game, a player with the local Kota Baru side had also attacked a spectator during the match, his punishment being a three-match ban. It turned out that Cantona's fame had not just been built on the Palace incident; this young boy seemed to know as much as any diehard Red. He described to me his goal of the season at Wimbledon, the effect the loss of Cantona had had on the United team and the prospects for United once he had returned to the side. He and his mates couldn't wait to watch his return against Liverpool live on TV in a couple of months' time. Here, 8,000 miles from Manchester, Cantona was a star – and the man who got me a second free burger.

Rimbaud

Of all the totemic devices cited to illustrate the 'other-ness' of Eric in regard to the norms of English footie, few have been as overworked as his love for the art and example of Arthur Rimbaud. Arthur's surname is pronounced 'Rambo', hence the two most infamous, and perhaps apocryphal, gags: Leeds fans flooding Eric's pigeon-hole with pics of Sly Stallone when they heard of his devotion to Rimbaud, and United colleagues responding 'Yeah, we've already seen *First Blood*' when Eric raised the subject of the poet. Ho ho ho. Sounds more like one of Choccy's heavily ironic witticisms to me, actually.

Still, poetry is a dangerous subject in which to admit an interest within the walls of an English dressing-room. After all, Graeme Le Saux risked life and limb merely through being seen with a copy of the *Guardian*, so being obsessed with the overwrought passionate poems of a nineteenth-century homosexual is hardly a recipe for laddish bonding. But Rimbaud, who died in 1891 after a tempestuous and debauched life of thirty-seven years, has influenced many a left-field rebel. Even the hard-bitten neo-psychos who created the CBGB punk scene in mid-1970s New York felt the pull, although admittedly it does appear that some were more attracted by Rimbaud's avant-garde and gravity-defying barnet than his spiritual stanzas. Thankfully, Eric hasn't opted for that particular hair-don't yet, a *faux pas* that even the House of Style (>>) would find hard to excuse.

It is quite apt that Eric should be drawn to poetry,

the purest and highest of the written-word art forms. Doesn't it form a trinity of purity with his other artistic choices: painting, the central visual art, and football, the ultimate physical spiritual expression? (Bugger ballet, of course: no Nureyev pirouette can match a Cantona pass.) It is even rumoured that there are Cantona poems in existence which he is too shy or modest to expose to public glare; examining the way he expresses himself in interviews, in epigrammatic style as though each sentence were a line from an epic poem, one can well believe it. As a Cantona hero, Rimbaud is placed at the top alongside Jim Morrison and his favourite footballers; indeed, one of Eric's most notorious quotes compares the Pelé–Alberto World Cup pass to the imagery of Rimbaud, claiming them both as 'expressions of beauty which give us a feeling of eternity'. As ever, Eric is drawn to that which brings immortality – he is driven to produce the on-field poetry that may one day inspire others to compare his passes to the art of legends. Some motivation: a rather different kind of win-bonus from that which English footie usually provides.

Those interested enough to find out what all the fuss is about can get Rimbaud's epic *A Season In Hell* for sixty pence. The story of a tortured soul's twisted spiritual journey, it could've been written for Eric's 1994/5 season. And Pam Ayres it ain't; there's even more evidence of drug-frenzy here than you'd find at Orient. Rimbaud lived hard 'n' fast and died still The Rebel (>>); how could Eric, knowing what we do about his predilections, be anything other than drawn to this turbulent spirit?

Ryan Giggs

Eric is the Sorcerer – then there's no doubt as to who's his Apprentice. The shared facets make the pairing inevitable: unbelievably precocious natural talent evident to all from the start; singled out at fourteen as the best of their age; under intense public and media scrutiny at all times; the constant battle to transform potential into achievement. Those who are so quick to criticize Giggs when he endures his spells of doubt and poor form should remember his age and recall that it wasn't until Eric was twenty-seven that he finally became a key champion player. Of course, Eric no longer needs a teacher or guide; one of the differences between him and Giggs is that, since leaving Auxerre, he's been essentially on his own – as a player, he's self-raised. Giggs is fortunate – he has Ferguson, Kidd and, surely above all, Eric. Dare you dream what Giggs might be capable of at twenty-seven?

Fergie once remarked that Giggs had a 'bullshit-filter' fitted inside his head, an instinct for immediately separating what will be good for him from the bad. It seems that he recognized the good in Eric from the moment he arrived. When Cantona's infamous extra training sessions began, Giggs was the first volunteer to join him and the keenest student. Whenever Giggs talks about Eric, his usual invariable monotone quivers in awe and admiration. Moreover, Eric's influence extends well beyond the pitch: just listen to Giggs purr over Eric's demeanour, his style, the way he holds himself, the way his radiating self-confidence creates an untouchable aura about him.

One cheeky pup once suggested that there was something homo-erotic about this but it's more like an older–younger brother relationship, the sort of fraternal idealizations you got in fifties US B-movies for teens. What makes Giggs so appealing is that he makes no cocky Manc-lad-swagger attempt to conceal his attitude. For Ferguson, this is an unexpected spin-off. Eric was supposed to be a selfish mercurial bad lad when he arrived, not a potential role model and teacher. Since Giggsy's first flush of pure instinctive brilliance came to an end as oppositions 'found him out', Fergie has worked endlessly on making him a full-range player. He used to tell him to watch Beckenbauer and Cruyff videos so that he would learn about vision, technique and control. 'Arrogance, authority and composure are factors a young player doesn't instinctively have', noted Fergie to Giggs. Now, instead of lifeless videos, Giggs can learn direct from a master of all three, from someone who has already pre-digested the lessons of Franz and his hero Johann for him. As Fergie remarked: 'All will come Ryan's way . . . if he occasionally looks up to learn a lesson or two in vision and passing from Eric Cantona.' During 1995/6, the fruits of these lessons have begun to emerge. Especially when handed his favourite free midfield role, Giggs now has a range of colours in his palette that enables him to work on the same canvas as Eric. If, God forbid, Eric ever leaves us, he will at least have left us the footballing equivalent of a son.

'S' is for . . .

Señor Miguel

. . . de Beswique, the pseudonymous artist, scriptwriter, would-be Sergio Leone, Red Issue *resident surrealist and football student who's seen a lot of changes since 1957. Not actually the slightest bit Spanish or French, he nevertheless trails the sulphur of Dali and Pablo as he stalks the Wild East mean streets of Beswick.*

When, for the third time in a year, the artist with the gypsy's soul lifted his proud head and drove a few more motorway miles in his own quest for footballing Nirvana, this time he changed direction, and headed west. And as he cruised along the M62 motorway, he finally saw his destiny – his true footballing home. A home where he would be loved unconditionally and where, through the wisdom and experience of his now-beloved manager Alex Ferguson, his inherent human flaws would be accepted as being part of the whole; where self-righteous judgement and hypocritical accusations would never, ever breathe life; where his unique genius would be recognized and acknowledged; where he would at last feel that he was dwelling among kindred spirits. That home was, of course, the imposing 'Theatre of Dreams'. And there, in December 1992, Monsieur Eric Cantona and Manchester United began their volatile, stupendous and most passionate love affair, which was to bear fruit within one season. Yes, 'Cantona is God' to the fans at Old Trafford. And any ball-park search for the reason why he has so securely captured the hearts and minds of United followers will produce a separate, distinct answer from everyone involved. To me personally, the answer is quite simple. Eric Cantona is a true man, as well as being a sublime, mercurial footballer.

This man Cantona is a rare breed in our modern, preconditioned, indolent, apathetic world-culture: he is a man who is totally true to, and at ease with, his own human nature, regardless of what it may cost him in the eyes of smaller, more oppressed, more narrow-minded souls. This young man genuinely would prefer to 'die on his feet, than live on his knees'. Such has been the power and ferocity of the media onslaught against one person – this solitary, polite, studious family man – that it was even to grotesque, hard-nosed bastards like myself a quite daunting, fearful and prolonged episode. And yet not once did Eric Cantona complain. Not once did he whine, or hide, or sell his 'story' to the newspapers, protesting a hapless, misguided innocence. Subjected to an appalling, megalomanic magistrate's quite vicious prison sentence for common assault, Cantona held his silence and maintained his dignity.

Watching it all unfold, it felt as if we were indeed living inside some Lewis Carroll nightmare. Ohhh, yes – it was, to quote all those 'fair game' tabloid headlines and all those symbols of perfection who present our televised soccer, quite 'shameful!'. It was indeed 'disgusting'. It was totally and absolutely 'disgraceful', truly a most 'appalling example to set before the young people of this nation'! But I know, and my two young sons know, and many other ordinary, common mortals also know, it wasn't the hot-headed, single-minded young man from Gaul who was deserving of such stomach-churning, scurrilous epithets, it was each and every single one of his acutely diminished, gratuitously malevolent detractors.

Being a mere man, Eric Cantona is quite easily capable of committing sin, of that there is no doubt; he is no angel. And, er, who among us is? This 'god' Eric Cantona is simply a man. And for his courage in standing by his beliefs in the face of overwhelming pressure, Eric Cantona is to me a true man. Not a bad footballer, either . . .

Spontaneity

When Eric is in full verbal flight, capturing the imagination with his visions of an ideal for living and playing, two almost interchangeable words continually shout for attention: spontaneity and instinct. He is, paradoxically, a thinking man who would not be insulted if you said he'd acted without thinking. Whereas so many Europeans come over here and decry our game because it doesn't allow time for considered reflection, Eric cheerfully professes to love the pressure and pace. Of course, 90 per cent of the time he is as careful and studied as any Gullit or Platini, creating space to give himself time to consider the odds. But it is that remaining ten per cent when spontaneous instinct takes over that he treasures; that is when the natural artist can reveal his superiority: 'I love the speed of the game, keeping the momentum going at all times; the spontaneity is beautiful.'

It is no accident that almost all of Cantona's heroes share the same belief and ability to improvise; you can see it in the ball-play of Cruyff, the volleys of McEnroe, the delivery of Brando and the performance of Morrison. For Eric, spontaneity is the offspring of two essential facets: natural artistic temperament and being in touch with the self. If, as Cantona always declares, one must be true to one's nature, then a willingness to trust one's basic instincts in a split-second decision is an unavoidable prerequisite. And in his opinion, the connection between spontaneity and art is umbilical but inseparable: 'Every artist tries to find spontaneity in what they do. The quest for it is fundamental and football expresses it best. Without spontaneity, you can't succeed.'

But there is also a philosophical basis to this credo. As Cantona has signed up to the Jean Jacques Rousseau (>>) concept of the 'Noble Savage', then it follows that he is driven to allow sentiment, emotion and momentary passion to override any restraints that reason or inhibition would impose. This is precisely the 'passion and fire' with which he plays that he concedes 'sometimes causes harm'; this is what he meant when he talked of the futility of trying to correct his behavioural instincts – remove the spontaneity which can release both good and bad and you separate the man from his self and his artistic soul. The instinctive, intuitive flash that gave us that Wimbledon volley and the pass to Irwin against Spurs can also result in kung-fu and stamping; it's a sort of Faustian bargain but one which most Red Devils are prepared to accept. And if it's an automatic instinct for self-preservation rather than deliberate and conscious behaviour-inhibition that's keeping him out of trouble for the time being, so much the better.

I guess that means those who tried to defend Eric's kung-fu as being 'out of character' were either being disingenuous or ignorant. Surely the point was that acting on instinct and being intolerant of attacks on his family are both exactly *in* character. What shocked the English mentality was his failure to keep a stiff upper lip; our phlegmatic character is built on suppressing instinct and maintaining our cool, hence our supposed distaste for 'hot-blooded and excitable' Latin temperaments. As Eric remarked long before Selhurst, 'People who accuse me of being disruptive forget I have my reasons – I'm trying to remain as instinctive as possible.' I always thought that his stamping on Moncur was far worse than Selhurst Park anyway; now that action truly did reveal the black edges of the heart. But then not even I would claim his nature is perfect. What does impress is his willingness to allow his spontaneity to reveal the good and bad about him to us. A man who loves his privacy has, in some senses, sacrificed much of it for the greater good of his art. (Can't see the FA disciplinary committee ever buying that as mitigation, unfortunately.) (>> the Inner Child, *Weltanschauung*)

Stade de Mosson

Mellifluous Montpellier, sweet centre of the south and a happy resonance for all Reds who danced around the Stade de Mosson and the Place de la Comédie in the spring of 1991. If Marseilles is the vibrant, proletarian, abrasive side of the Midi, then Montpellier is the turned cheek: soft, lush, well-to-do, laid back. Eighty miles down the road from the Vélodrome, at once close enough for the succours of home yet sufficiently distanced from the turmoil of Tapie and his henchmen. A place to recover and rediscover, so Eric might have thought. As it happened, his season in exile contained more crisis and drama than he expected.

En route, he stopped off at Bordeaux, seeing out the last four months of the 1988/9 season. Delighted to be under the tutelage of World Cup hero Jean Tigana, he repaired his wounds with the balm of six goals in eleven starts before taking a 50 per cent pay cut to move on further loan to the Hérault club for the 1989/90 season. In a weird parallel, Montpellier proceeded to endure, then enjoy, precisely the same season as United did back in England; fitting, then, that we should have met in 1990/1. Club president Nicollin and coach Aimé Jacquet had assembled some star names – Eric, his old Under-21 mate Stéphane Paille, Valderrama, Laurent Blanc and Julio César. But just as the Reds found, star names did not immediately a star team make. Whilst United plunged towards the foot of the table via that derby defeat, Montpellier followed suit by way of their own particular trauma – Eric kicking off in the dressing-room in the very same week that we lost 5–1 (>> Violence). For both clubs, the Cup was to offer a lifeline.

At first, Eric despaired. Once again he had to struggle to build his own career within a construction that was shaking to the foundations. The threat of scapegoating loomed once more – a management which had raised a town's expectations but not delivered would need its sacrificial victim. But in the wake of the Cantona–Lemoult bust-up, when a Tapie might have had Eric dropped off a bridge in concrete boots, Nicollin held back. Eric returned within ten days and a slow but sure recovery began. He had, at last, been shown some faith and understanding: that's all he ever asks for. By the spring, the club was safe and embarked on a Cup run as Valderrama and Eric fed hungrily off each other's balls, so to speak. A last sixteen hat-trick and a quarter-final pair from Eric propelled his name on to the back pages and into the songs of the Mosson *garçons*. Montpellier had never won the merest bauble before; Eric, who had left Auxerre in the tears of a Cup defeat, now sensed he was on the verge of emulating his OM heroes of '76. At St Etienne in the semi, Eric remarked that he was truly in his element: death or glory on a moment's instinct. That moment came for him – the sweetest volley for the winning goal.

Like United, they faced a team in their own city for the final, Matra Racing, the team he had almost been swayed to join. Like United, they had to battle through extra-time but managed to win on the day itself, 2–1. Eric, just turned twenty-four, had his first major medal. Marvelling at the sheer drama of the final on the

Champs-Élysées later that night, roistering with colleagues against whom he had squared up back in September, he was asked if he had proved something to OM
and the world with this comeback in exile. He merely
smiled that sardine-trawler smirk and turned back to his
Veuve Clicquot: to ask the question was to supply the
answer. (>> Nimes)

Symbolism

The French and Continentals in general love symbolism
in their art. Indeed, there was a time when virtually
every piece of European cinema entailed the viewer
scratching his head and wondering what the hell the
various red boxes, strange asides and significant fixed
shots were supposed to mean. In the Cantona context,
symbolism has a slightly altered definition. When he is
unable to communicate with us directly, he declares what
he has to say through gestures and actions; thankfully
they're a good deal easier to decode than those in
obscure Scandinavian art films. Here are the top ten
examples complete with translation.

1. SPITTING ON AN ELLAND ROAD WALL
(not at a fan)
While he could not bring himself to spit upon them
personally because he still appreciates what they meant
to him, he registered his disgust at their Munich songs,
psychotic hostility and blame-shifting management by
despoiling their council home.

2. COCKING HIS FINGERS AT BLACKBURN FANS

His brilliant winning goal had blown away their title
hopes and shot through their jumped-up pretensions,
the *nouveaux riches sacs à merdes*. Well, until Wednesday
anyway.

3. DRESSING CASUAL FOR FIRST COURT APPEARANCE

He laughs in the face of danger and farts in its general
direction (etc). He will not be cowed into conforming
to tinpot authority and if this was good enough for Mr
Prince, it's good enough for Mrs Pearch.

4. WEARING A TIE FOR THE RETURN FIXTURE

He takes nothing back of what he said last time but Mr
Watkins bought him the tie especially and started crying
hysterically when Eric looked doubtful.

5. CUPPING AN EAR TO RIVAL FANS AFTER GOAL

'Ha! What was that you were singing about my mother,
fils des putains?'

6. ONE ARM ALOFT AFTER SCORING AT CITY

Was that as good as a Denis Law or what? Just call him
Eric The King.

7. SHAVING HIS HEAD BEFORE MATCH AT BREST

'I want to feel the fresh rain and the strength of the
wind on my skull,' was how he explained it at the time.
Nothing to do with the headlines helping him get
noticed by the Under-21 selectors, of course.

8. SHAVING HIS HEAD BEFORE MATCH AT OT

Surely simultaneously a symbol of embarking on a fresh start as a changed man as well as a visual reminder to the opposition hackers that he's a hard bastard 'criminal' who'll take no nonsense.

9. ROARING HUGHESIE-LIKE TO HEAVENS AFTER GOAL AT NEWCASTLE

This is as important a goal as that 1985 semi-final winner; no need to hang back with cool modesty so let it rip.

10. KUNG-FU KICK AT SELHURST PARK

The ultimate dual Commandment symbol: Kick Racism Out Of Football and Honour Thy Father And Thy Mother. Probably not, as 'House of Style' might suggest, a necessary fashion statement about leather jackets with ties.

'T' is for . . .

Terry Lloyd

Every earthquake trails its aftershocks, although it's unusual for them to occur as far away as Guadeloupe is from Thornton Heath. As Eric and the family relaxed at the Club Med a fortnight after Selhurst Park, ITN, a supposedly serious news organization, thought it in the public interest for a reporter to fly out and confront him and his pregnant wife. Such is the sort of editorial mentality that makes the three main ITV bulletins such a pile of pants; clearly anyone at ITN with any taste gets sent to Channel 4 News. Officially, this never happened: Eric was alleged to have kung-fu kicked Lloyd in the chest after being pestered on the beach and to have thrown in some blood-curdling verbals for good measure. The police turn up, confiscate the film and threaten Lloyd with prosecution for breaching the French-style privacy laws. So far, so funny. But this is the cool bit: within seconds of completing his 'assault', a becalmed Eric turns round, signs an autograph for a fan and starts chatting politely with admiring on-lookers as Lloyd staggers away. Tarantinian or what? Like blowing someone's head off as an aside before continuing a discussion of Madonna's hamburger preferences.

Much was later made of Lloyd's credentials, a veteran of Bosnia, the Arctic and other hell-holes; strange then that he should be so ignorant of the island's culture that he thought he could trample all over their privacy laws with impunity. For once, authority had not thrown Eric to the wolves; as fellow holiday-makers pointed out, 'we all believe in the French ways here'. The French and Eric are proud that their laws safeguard a man's privacy; for some reason the English, for all their bluster about liberty and their home being their castle, do not.

Lloyd's actions seemed symbolic of the way even the 'respectable' media behaved over Eric, dragged down by market forces and the tabloids' pull to depths they should never touch. And by running home squealing, Lloyd didn't look much of a man compared to the family-defending Cantona; it was a sign of the changing national sentiment that much of the ensuing press comment supported Eric. But what I found most reprehensible was Lloyd's subsequent assertion that he was a United fan. Leave aside the fact that no true Red would call his daughter Chelsey as Lloyd did, what sort of man would put his job ahead of his club? Having dealt with many media types over the last couple of years, it is remarkable how many claim to be Reds yet engage in activities that do harm to the Red cause. Some protest that they've got to do what they're told but what sort of defence is that? Old Trafford is full of lads who've lost jobs, wages, bonuses or promotions simply because they refuse to miss matches – it never occurs to them to do otherwise.

Terry Lloyd chose to accept the Cantona mission; a few bruised ribs may well be seen as a lucky escape.

Therapy

'**W**here's Yer Marbles?'; 'Nutcase!'; 'Mad Eric'; 'The Lunatic's Lunge'; suddenly, after Selhurst Park, every tabloid sub-editor is a mental health specialist. What a pity Eric doesn't seem to have heard of ex-minister John Patten getting successfully sued by an educationalist he'd called a 'nutter' – The *Sun* vs Monsieur Cantona could have been some libel case.

Doubtless the papers thought they were being funny when they dragged in several rent-a-quote headshrinks to 'diagnose' Eric. In fact being on the couch is nothing new for Cantona, nor is it something he's the slightest bit embarrassed about – the French and English are very different when it comes to doctors and health. France, to be blunt, is a nation of hypochondriacs and pharmaceutical junkies, a weekly visit to the doc considered as normal as the Saturday trip to the bordello. The classic Brit, however, would rather die quietly without a fuss than be examined by the men in white coats. No self-respecting Englishman would be seen anywhere near Susie Orbach's clinic; the French take the American view that you'd have to be mad *not* to go to a shrink.

Eric was only just into his twenties when he first began visiting psychoanalysts. Not that he had any particular problems; it was merely that his interest in dreams and Jungian theory, an interest he shared with many of his heroes like Morrison, had incited him to attempt some consciousness-raising and examination of the subconscious mind. One of his analysts was later to suggest that England would be the best place for him to thrive; Eric chose Marseilles but later wryly remarked that he should've let his *id* overrule his *ego*.

He had a taste of what was to come in England after the Sedan shirt-throwing incident. French TV hired a shrink to construct a Cantona profile, no doubt hoping for all sorts of sensational demons to be revealed. Instead, he produced a glowing portrait of a model citizen – indeed, a lone, sane, intelligent paragon amid a sea of sickness and corruption. Eric was reported to be tickled pink by this and turned on his detractors who still held that he was bonkers: 'Anyone who is different is considered crazy so I am happy to be so considered. And proud.' The *Sun* got similarly disappointing results when they pulled the same stunt in 1995, but never let the facts interfere with a good story, hey? The press continue to be fascinated with the possibility that Cantona may in any way be 'defective'. The old story that Eric had undergone Tomates method speech therapy to correct a minor defect was disinterred; others flew the kite that bizarre blood sugar levels were to blame, even though that had long since been discounted. In all such attempts, you can hear the echoes of Victoriana, when free spirits with disconcerting ideals got sectioned away in Bedlam. Thankfully, the only lunatic asylum Eric's been inside is Elland Road.

Thespianism

If there's one mix worse than acting and pop stars, then it must be acting and footballers: *Escape To Victory* – need one say more? But just as Frank Sinatra was the exception that proved the rule as regards crooners on screen, will Eric turn out to fulfil that same role for footie stars? However much the media may have guffawed when it was announced Eric had won a part in *Le Bonheur Est Dans Le Pré*, there is much evidence to suggest that this was a natural step for our man to take.

His admiration for certain actors is well documented; leaving aside the childhood Bruce Lee infatuation, his top five are Gérard Depardieu and Isabelle Adjani from France, De Niro, Rourke and Brando from the States. Tellingly, the Method School influence looms large in his selection. Such actors approach their craft in the same way as Eric does his: they 'train' relentlessly, honing and practising performances; they concentrate on motivation and projecting performance rather than letting the texts of others predominate, just as Eric revels in the free role unconstrained by tactical strait-jackets. Cantona's favourite methods of improvisation and spontaneity, disdained by the classical actors, are embraced by the Method men; moreover, the immersion within the role that allows such actors to reinvent their image spectacularly has always appealed to those of an existential bent such as Eric.

As for image projection and camera-friendliness, Eric's try-outs in advertising – don't knock it, this is where every modern English director learns his trade – have demonstrated he has little to learn. The louche cool of his naughty Nike ad, the superb eye-to-camera steeliness of his anti-racism spot, the remarkable camp comedy of his naked shower scene in the French 'Bic' promotion – all illustrations of natural screen presence. Add to all this his recurrent rhetoric about 'performance', 'image' and 'drama' and you have a man who's clearly just waiting for that directorial call.

That it should have come from Etienne Chatiliez was some honour: his 1990 breakthrough hit *Tatie Danielle*, a tart black comedy about a malicious old cow, had made him one of French cinema's brightest hopes. In *Le Bonheur*, Eric plays a rough rugby player called Lionel who's married with kids but has put a local capitalist's daughter up the duff. Obviously, he's not the lead but he gets a remarkable amount of screen-time for a novice and stands up well next to the superb veteran star Michel Serrault. If you're going to be picky, then his Marseilles accent ill fits a character born and bred in Gers, but then De Niro never altered his patter much either. (Did you hear Bob's Jewish accent in *Once Upon A Time* . . . ? No, nor did I.) The film has been a major hit in France, garlanded with critical awards including Césars; Chatiliez spoke enthusiastically about Eric's acting which could be described as eighties De Niro, part Method part character. 'He stands in front of the camera like he's about to take a penalty. Total motivation – you can see him thinking "shit, I've got to score". He is a truthful natural, like a character from Pagnol.' How Eric must have purred reading that: Marcel Pagnol is possibly his favourite novelist whose books summon up the definitive images of Eric's home region. Can a role for Eric in a sequel to *Le Château de Ma Mére* be far away?

Tony J

*R*ed *Issue contributor, forthcoming author and friend to the stars, Tony J recalls that magical night when Red phone lines burned hot and stricken Sheep howled: 'Remember, remember, the end of November.'*

Friday 26 November 1992: Manchester United signed Eric Cantona from Leeds United for £1m. Just like adults over the age of forty-five can remember where they were when President Kennedy was assassinated, United fans can recall their exact whereabouts when the news of that shock transfer broke.

I returned home from work a little later than usual that night and the in-car entertainment had consisted of listening to tapes rather than the early evening news. I had two answer-machine messages that night. One from a mate called Geoff, saying rather agitatedly, 'Tony, pick up the phone . . . okay, I'll phone you later,' and another from my brother Billy that simply said: 'Tony, press 141 on Teletext when you get in, then phone me.' What could it be, I wondered? Obviously footie-related, but what? Fergie resigns? Robson retires? Man City buy shares in Duraglit? On seeing the headline I had to sit down: 'Cantona signs for Manchester United'.

My mind was racing. Why would Leeds sell us their best player? Why was the fee such a steal? He must be a crock. He must be a disruptive influence and Wilkinson wants rid at any price. He might be a bit Turtle. Is the Teletext editor on a complete wind-up? Did BT sponsor the story knowing every United fan in the world would be phoning every other United fan in the world in a desperate attempt to find out what was going on? I phoned my brother for a twenty-minute discussion; I phoned Geoff for a thirty-minute discussion; I phoned Mick for a twenty-minute discussion . . .

Finally it occurred to me to phone someone who might actually know a bit more than us Red Mancs. I have a colleague in Leeds called Ian, a big Leeds fan but fortunately not that bitter. I had long admired Ian's ability to hold an intelligent discussion on football without foaming at the mouth at the mere mention of Manchester United, an ability sadly not shared by the overwhelming majority of his fellow Leeds fans. His phone was constantly engaged for over two hours. I finally got through and he wasn't as pleased to hear my voice as he normally was. 'Ringing up to gloat about Cantona are you?' was his first response. I assured him I merely wanted some information on what was going on. I had apparently interrupted him in the middle of composing a letter to the *Yorkshire Evening Post* on the subject of why Leeds had sold the wrong player to the wrong club at the wrong price.

After eventually calming down a little, Ian launched into chapter and verse about just how fantastic United's new purchase was and how he failed to believe that Wilkinson could be so stupid as to sell him at any cost. I could remember seeing Cantona single-handedly destroy the Scousers in the Charity Shield so I knew he was a bit special, but I still had to ask Ian why he considered Cantona's loss such a cruel blow. He replied by saying, 'Wait until you see him play regularly; he just does things.' 'What do you mean, he just does things?' I replied. 'You'll see – he just does things.'

Eric made his first appearance on 6 December 1992 in the derby game. My first real glimpse of the majesty that is King Eric came moments after he calmly entered the cacophonous maelstrom that masquerades as a local footballing contest in these parts. Cantona picked the ball up near the touchline and released the most magnificently weighted pass seen on the hallowed turf in years. It split the stuttering Blue defence, leaving the recipient of the pass, Brian McClair, and the rest of us in no doubt about the mouthwatering prospect of watching Monsieur Cantona on a regular basis. You were right Ian, my sheep-following chum: he just does things, doesn't he mate? And unfortunately for you and every other football fan who doesn't follow United, he does it in a Red shirt and he does it better than anybody else.

'U' is for . . .

'United We Stand'

*W*hat was once Red Issue's *young brother is now into its second half-century and one of the nation's top-selling 'zines. Editor* Andy Mitten *looks back from his office on the feverish times of 1995.*

Wednesday, 9 August 1995. A dreadful day. How could such an innocent-looking balmy Mancunian morning turn out to be such a killer? I was so contented, full of enthusiasm for the new season after the summer sorties. There was a pre-season game away at Bradford that very evening to look forward to. Then it happened – a double-whammy, in tabloid-speak.

It wasn't the girl I'd stayed faithful to deciding she was better off with a cockney she'd met behind my back on holiday. No, it was the man I'd stuck by with unequalled passion deciding he was better off in Paris. He'd had enough: he wanted out. The bastards had ground him down. Girls come and go, geniuses don't. I was emotionally sapped. For close on seven months, I'd defended the man to whom many had attached the label 'indefensible'. Not once had I condoned his actions at Selhurst Park but I and every other real United fan thought there was more than a case for the defence. United were chasing a League and Cup Double but one man was dictating the pages of *UWS*, a man who wasn't even in the team. He was on the cover, in articles, all over the letters pages. Each letter or article was a variation on one theme – that real United fans were unanimous in support for our king.

We had our detractors all right. The hysterical tabloid media tried to corral impartial Joe Public into believing that he really should be jailed and banned from football for life. Was being hanged, drawn and quartered really too good for our Gallic god? People who genuinely didn't have a clue about football were trying to tell us the score. This wasn't an issue for football, they were even talking about it on Richard and Judy. The editor of a Crystal Palace fanzine tried to tell me and the listening millions on Radio Five Live that the death of a Palace fan in Birmingham was a direct consequence of his actions at Selhurst Park. Give me strength . . .

It was worth it though. The light never did go out and by the close season it was rather more than a distant dim. That's why I was so gutted on 9 August. All those tireless hours spent convincing people that he should stay were wasted. He saw sense though, changed his mind and made a triumphant return to doing what he does best: playing in the red shirt of Manchester United. Eric Cantona? The best by far.

'U Or Non-U?'

Nancy Mitford's infamous phrase, and the 1930s book it spawned, encapsulates the most crippling division in English society: not necessarily that between the moneyed and the skint but between the two class-based universes of taste which define what Jarvis Cocker calls the 'common' and the 'nice'. The English capacity for endlessly inventing new forms of snobbery would be very impressive if it were not so pathetic. As Orwell sadly reflected, 'No Englishman can open his mouth without giving cause for another to despise him.' When you consider that many still seriously believe the usage of 'serviette' instead of 'napkin' marks out the sort of kid they don't want at their darling offspring's school, the fact that this society united to win the war seems even more miraculous. The French, despite their nominal egalitarianism, aren't immune to this either: to hear a member of the BCBG upper-crust refer witheringly to the *ouvrier* classes' taste as *concièrge* leaves one in no doubt.

Therefore it is one of Eric's most endearing features that he has risen above this cross-Channel mindset; in some ways he epitomizes the ideal of classless society citizenship in which John Major once famously professed to believe. If you examine in English sociological terms the journey he has made from milieu to milieu, it could be characterized as a classic aspirational generation movement, from 'pure' proletarian origins in a traditional working-class environment to a lifestyle that is bourgeois both in terms of income bracket and cultural indicators.

He earns close to £20,000 a week, reads *The Times*, patronizes fine-art galleries and art-house cinemas and married 'above himself' (as the loathsome phrase has it). Men who have 'risen' in such a fashion usually exhibit two behavioural features: firstly, they can bring with them a chippy sense of a latent inferiority complex; secondly, as in the Michael Caine syndrome, they may seek either to kick the ladder away or disparage the mentality of those they have left behind.

Cantona suffers from neither affliction. Indeed, he has reversed the normal model, at least that which is the norm in football. Not for him the conspicuous consumption, flash boy-racer motors and precious celeb-behaviour of your average pro. And while preening jack-the-lads swan about in the sort of glitzy gear that screams 'loadsamoney for this schmutter, pal', Eric always settles for the cool understatement that is true class.

A perfect illustration is his choice of housing. Generally, the first thing players do when they make it big is splash out on a horrendous mock-something pile in the stockbroker belt; as with Oasis, the 'working-class hero' can't wait to escape the working-class world that made him the man he is in the first place. Eric did precisely the opposite, choosing to move to a nondescript Leeds suburb where he positively welcomed being surrounded by Asian and Afro-Caribbean working-class neighbours, just the sort of environment those in the flight to Wilmslow are desperate to escape. When he finally moved to Manchester, he again plumped for suburban ordinariness by settling in an unprepossessing Booths-town housing estate, the most unlikely destination for those seeking wealthy superstars. And when he fancied a drink he spurned the jumped-up 'exclusive' bars in Manchester's hotels for the local public saloon at the Bridgewater.

It is ironic, given his aloof and untouchable aura on the pitch, that he is one of the most approachable and visible players in the city; it seems to be a result of a deliberate attempt not to allow his wealth and status to separate him from everyday reality.

Ian Ridley quotes a Cantona acquaintance as sneering the dread phrase 'champagne socialist' in describing Eric. Actually, its hard to see any evidence of Cantona financial extravagance; he may not lead the life of an ascetic but his lifestyle is hardly on a level with those of the Antonia Frasers, John Mortimers and Barbara Follets of that Hampstead-centred world. If he is proud to call himself a socialist – yes, the 's' word is still allowed in France – then what difference does his income make anyway? Or should, as a corollary, the working classes be banned from voting Tory? Isn't it telling how hostile the moneyed classes become when one of their own suggests that there is more to care about in life than oneself?

Utopia

Thomas More missed out a couple of details in his vision of Utopia. Throw in a Theatre of Dreams, a Frenchman who is a personification of a brotherhood's ideals, and a couple of million ecstatic worshippers and that would be more like it. It's obvious that Eric has been a Utopian figure for us Reds (that is what much of this book is about). Mancunians, by and large, are not people prone to gushing; they tend to ration out approval sparingly, ever ready to cut the swollen-headed down to size. But they've abandoned all normal reserve with Eric.

But what have we in turn meant to Cantona? The culture of England, and of English football in particular, is not supposed to be conducive to the Continental. Yet Eric has become as much of an Anglophile as a proud Frenchman can be. The very features of our game that Europeans so often disparage are precisely what he loves: the speed, power, devotion to committed attacking and the intense pressure from the fans. He makes the connection with his own belief in spontaneity and beauty: when the pace is helter-skelter, instinct becomes the most important sense; when ceaseless attacking movement is demanded, the artist has the opportunity to be beautiful. And for a man who believes in performance, what better stage than our theatrical stadiums with their passionate, engaged audiences?

Furthermore, he seems to enjoy the English character. The discovery that, at least here in the north, we are nothing like the cool and distant stereotype Europe would have us be, has come as a revelation; he admires our patriotism, our pragmatism and our doggedness, even the much maligned methods with which we educate our kids. And naturally enough, he likes us for liking him: 'Here, they're not afraid to tell me they love me.' But he could find that at any English club. Manchester United gives him something else, a city he realizes is special and a club whose values uniquely connect with his. Someone once labelled Eric a footballing adulterer, which was a slack analogy; in fact, he has been a relentlessly serial monogamist, careful never to propose marriage. At Old Trafford, he has reached the stage where he can dare to say this: 'I am in love with United. It is like finding a wife who has given me the perfect marriage.' We Reds have played our part in wooing him, and when he re-signed he was professing a loyalty to the fans as much as the club or its individuals. As his famous quote has it, 'I feel close to the rebelliousness and vigour of youth here . . . behind Manchester's windows, there is an insane love of football, celebration and music.'

It's obvious too that the practicalities of being at United have worked well for him: he has a team that is built around him, that plays the way he wants, commanded by men who give him the respect and, yes, love that he always sought but was denied: 'I value truth, honesty, respect, compassion and understanding – I have found these qualities at Manchester United.' So an outsider in a foreign land has somehow made a true home here. At Old Trafford he gets an environment of love, respect and faith that he hasn't had since he left his Caillols cave. This, perhaps, is his Utopia: that he is finally among brothers who share his sacred family values.

'V' is for . . .

'Venue of Legends'

. . . as Wembley is laughably self-dubbed; fans might substitute 'Venue of Piss-Pools, Bollock-Burgers and Shite-Sight Seats'. For the foreigner, however, Wembley's kudos has somehow remained untarnished. Hard-bitten foreign mercenaries, blasé from weekly performances in Milan or Madrid, still babble excitedly when the prospect of an appearance in salubrious Brent occurs. Klinsmann was apparently prepared to spend a year in the grottier parts of Norf Landan just to get the chance of playing in a Cup final (nowt to do with the twenty grand a week, of course). For Eric, ever in thrall to legend, romanticism and historic deeds, Wembley retains its purity and he's had the good fortune to play there seven times since his arrival in England. Supposedly beside himself with excitement on the morning before his first club appearance there, in which he scored a Charity Shield hat-trick for Leeds, he must have later reflected with bitter irony that a ban slammed as 'lenient' by others should cost such a prize as a probable second Cup winners' medal.

Wembley is made for men such as Cantona. The pitch

rolls true for the artist's passes, the expansive nature of the stage perfect for the natural performer. Wembley may be pompous on its grand occasions but that's all the better to bring the ego to the fore. He's done his cameos and pulled some party-pieces in our two Charity Shield victories there, practising his penalties along the way; he's had the required Wembley let-down too that sharpens the appetite for the next time. In the original Ides Of March aftermath, that League Cup Final was never his for the taking; the flip suggestion would be that a Fizzy Pop Bauble is beneath him anyway. But Cantona at Wembley signals one seismic date above all: May the fourteenth, 1994, and the FA Cup Final.

It had been a strange first-half. Eric looked slightly bemused by the disjointed rhythms, the odd ungainly movements of both sides. You could sense the scribblers getting ready to write him off: 'Eric flops on the big day again.' But within a quarter-hour of the restart, with United rejuvenated and kicking towards the massed Red brigades, the only Eric flop on sight was his hairstyle collapsing under the sheeting drizzle. As he took up those familiar puppeteer's strings from his deep position, United began to dance; the defining moments duly arrived on sixty and sixty-six. No disrespect to the ageing stalwarts, but weren't you glad we now had Eric to call upon at times such as these rather than Choccy or Brucey? In this modern amphitheatre, Cantona had his prized gladiatorial moments; cool, composed and calculating, the drama offset by an ad lib comedic routine with the taxi-driver's favourite, he appeared not to feel an ounce of pressure, not a sweat-bead of anticipation.

The sheer arrogant cheek of twice selecting exactly the same square of net for aim somehow summed up both his and the team's season: untouchable class, whatever the weather. And Eric had rightly taken his place alongside Aston, Whiteside and Hughes at the Venue of Legends. (>> Epilogue)

Violence

In the bright, Brave New World of the family-fun game, you cannot risk being seen to offer the slightest justification for any form of footie-related violence. Do so and every self-appointed moral guardian, along with carpet-bagging twats like Johnny Dee, will jump all over you. It's a form of self-censorship that all those newcomer parasites are happy to impose; there is a terror shared by all those who've rushed to exploit the game since 1990 that gut opinions of traditional fans might be exposed, 'tarnishing' football's image and thus reducing profitability for all concerned.

Nevertheless, the truth remains, however much concealed. And in the matter of Eric Cantona's record of violence, the fact is that a large proportion of his following admires and approves of his 'hardness' and his ultimate willingness to express his anger physically. Not that Eric is essentially a violent man; not for him the routine Saturday night thuggery exhibited by some of his contemporaries, nor does his speech contain the tiresome threatening macho swagger of so many nineties 'lads'. Indeed, the hoariest old Eric quote is the one about passion and fire harming him and others; he is no apologist for brutality. Nonetheless, he has a track record of 'bundles' which are detailed below. The classic intellecto-pacifist argument would be that if Eric is supposed to be so sensitive, intelligent and self-possessed, resorting to violence is in fact an admission of inadequacy. That perhaps ignores the centrality of the instinctive spontaneity in Eric's character which can seize the initiative before the brain can engage. But on a more basic level, those on the receiving end have often asked for it and been given a taste of the only language they understand. Sorry to sound like a taxi-driver there, but rational intellectual responses can be pointless when dealing with pond-life (cf Selhurst Park, Pasadena Rose Bowl). So here are Eric's greatest hits – quite literally, Smashie – complete with advocate's defence.

1978: During an Under-13s match at Auxerre, young Eric has a running battle with a particularly Vinnie-ish defender: after a gruesome hack from behind, Eric explodes and an apparently vicious fist-fight ensues which has the staff worried about his temperament for weeks afterwards. Eight years later, the protagonists meet again in a first-team Auxerre-Nantes match: both are in the bath well before time.
Defence: too young to be held criminally responsible anyway. Provocation. And you always get let off for a first-time offence, right?

1983: The infamous Magnificent Seven Massacre. It appears players are just as susceptible as fans to seeing a car park as a fight-ring *manqué*. After an Auxerre reserve match, seven opponents wait for the home team's star at the car park entrance. Despite being warned of Eric's shoot-out prowess by Sheriff Guy Roux, the seven stand their ground, doubtless expecting the coward's odds to favour them with victory. Instead, Eric emerges in a whirlwind of kung-fu kicks and karate chops, flooring four of them within five seconds and putting the others to flight. A groundsman observer is said to have remarked with bewildered approval as the injured four sloped off to the club infirmary: 'If I'd seen that in the cinema, I wouldn't have believed it.'

Defence: doesn't even warrant a reference to the CPS. Self-defence and the use of minimum necessary force in doing so; had he been in uniform, would have merited some sort of medal.

1987: Eric shows his generally overlooked humility by mucking in with the young lads and apprentices to clear the snow from Auxerre's pitch. Bruno Martini, the goal-keeper and French international club star, is standing around doing little, a fact upon which Eric remarks. Martini drops a spleen-load of abuse on Eric's head, to which Eric replies with a swift right-hander to the eye socket.

Defence: a routine event at any English club. Provo-cation if Madame Cantona was mentioned. Worth no more than a fine, m'lud, which is exactly what he got: Guy Roux would make a better magistrate than Mrs Pearch, perhaps.

1989: The oft-repeated rumour is that Eric once

punched Marseilles president Bernard Tapie at the climax of a heated, personal argument involving much mutual insult. Eric was on his way within days, adding to the circumstantial evidence, and their loathing of each other is well documented. Tapie is notorious for his gigantic mouth which has got himself into plenty of trouble so you can hazard a guess that whatever he said to Eric was at a Simmonds level.

Defence: no proof anything happened. Almost certain provocation and possibly a pre-emptive strike. And given the state of the relationship between Tapie and the French judiciary, no *juge d'instruction* would ever let a Tapie complaint proceed anyhow. Not that he could afford to press the case any more either, tee-hee.

1990: Tough September days at Montpellier as Nicollin's dream team fails to click. In the dressing room, Jean Claude Lemoult remarks to a team-mate behind Eric's back that it's all the striker's fault. Eric swirls round and clumps his boots into Lemoult's face, sparking an all-in brawl. His Stade de Mosson days seem numbered as half a dozen players sign an anti-Eric round robin, but all is resolved with a smacked bottom and fine.

Defence: Lemoult was possibly asking for it by questioning a proud professional's application behind his back, but the use of boots as a weapon is hard to wriggle out of; blame heat-of-moment instinct and throw oneself at judge's mercy. Fortunately, French cases take aeons to come to judgement. In the meantime, Lemoult and Eric became pals so any proceedings would have been terminated by a cooked-up joint plea of 'we were just horsing about/he accidentally headbutted my Reeboks', etc.

1991: Threw ball at referee's legs whilst playing for Nimes (>> Authority): scarcely violent and something even saintly Ray Wilkins enjoys doing. Case dismissed.

1994: Contretemps at Swindon and Norwich away (>> Julius Caesar)

1994: Immovable, and intensely annoying, object meets irresistible force at the Pasadena Rose Bowl. Completely over-the-top jobsworth security at the World Cup so enrages the entire media that most are only too pleased when Eric gives one a slap for refusing to let him get on with his commentary job.
Defence: a clear case of the only language officious pedants understand. In any case, LA is the last place a jury is going to take the word of their notorious law enforcers over that of a celebrity football player, right OJ?

1995: Terry Lloyd (>>) and Selhurst Park. Of the latter, enough already. If you've bought this hagiographic book and read this far without throwing up in disgust, then you must be as much of a Cantonista as me; consequently, you know every post-Selhurst justification by heart because you also spent nine months repeating and refining them. I refer you to Richard Williams's one-liner (>> The *Guardian*) for the ultimate objective judgement. Well, almost objective.

181

'W' is for . . .

Weltanschauung

Another of those unspellable but handy German compound words, meaning philosophy of life or personal world-view. Some of this book has been an attempt to define the elements of the Cantona *Weltanschauung*: there's his existentialism tempered by a faith in his inner child nature; his adherence to spontaneous instinct and individualism; his championing of beautiful artistry and maintaining morality in the face of Mammon; his belief in the testing values of challenge and change over static conformity. But there is a final element that brings all the others together which is to some minds the most contentious: Cantona's belief that football is an art, not merely a sport, and that some within it deserve to be seen as artists.

Back to basic principles. As an existentialist, Eric knows that he is 'condemned to be free' and will be defined by his deeds. He must make a commitment, an engagement, to give his freedom a purpose. He has been lucky: he has been 'situated' in the world in such a way as to give him a natural, essential talent and this physical, genetic inheritance has been bolstered by the best possible familial environment. But he still needed to make the free existential choice to make the very most of his essential gifts and he has done that by abandoning his idyllic home and never giving in to the hostile forces that have blighted his career. His commitment, which has been his mission throughout his career, is to demonstrate that it is possible to be an artist in a profession dominated by functionalists. ('What is a functional person worth compared to an impassioned one?') Do so on one's own terms and never be untrue to one's self; raise football, in the eyes of those who wish to see it, to the level of an art form. And though he has never sought to be a role model, his example will nonetheless inspire others. He can thus leave an unforgettable legacy, for he knows death is truly final, not only for the sake of his name and his family's but for those who seek to learn from his example.

That's my theory and, unless Eric himself tells me it's deep-fried bollocks, I'm sticking to it. In the meantime, the final words on the subject must be Eric's as he discourses on his favourite subject of football's art.

Football is the most beautiful of arts. One day those who make football will have to understand that there is no salvation without the artist. The image of football is of sweat and muscles . . . but I dream of lightness, harmony and pleasure; I am looking for a symphony. When you are taught beauty at an early age, it is very difficult to give it up: a good footballer is by nature a beautiful footballer. Football inspires emotions that you cannot experience anywhere else, even in writing a great masterpiece. It is my passion, it's what I love most and it is art. (>> Zodiac)

Jim White

*A*uthor *of the highly recommended portrait of the modern United,* Are You Watching Liverpool?, *White is one of the last survivors at the* Independent *and one of the very few national journalists who understands the existential crisis of the traditional football supporter. On hand to witness the bestialities in Istanbul, here he recalls Eric's particular contribution to that twenty-four hours of lunacy.*

When United drew Galatasaray in the 1993/4 European Cup, a friend sent me a postcard saying 'what a draw'. It was, it seemed, a certain passport to the mini-league: trips to Milan, Monte Carlo and Moscow lay the other side of formality. Over-confidence always has its come-uppance. The banners unfurled by locals at Istanbul airport as the official party arrived read 'Welcome To Hell', and it was barely hyperbole: everywhere Reds were abused, deported, imprisoned. The stadium itself appeared to have been occupied by the mad bastard offspring of Saddam Hussein with a limited but fundamental grasp of English ('F*ck you Manchester', they chanted); you could see the United players visibly wilt under the noise and constant choking firework smoke. Worse, it was one of those games when Fergie's selection policy was at its most baroque: stymied he may have been by the three-foreigner regulation but to leave Hughes brooding on the bench seemed an act of unnecessary folly.

So Cantona was left alone up front. Or rather he wasn't left alone – his every step was shadowed by his German marker Stumpf. Up there, no one passed to him (to be fair, no one had the ball to pass it, Galatasaray being something none of us considered possible before-hand, a good side). You could see the fury building up inside his chest as nothing went right for United across the ninety minutes and the prospect of getting his hands on major silverware disappeared before his eyes. Five minutes from the end, the ball went into the mêlée of Turks – substitutes, officials, policemen – who had annexed the touchline running track. They thought it was very grown-up and clever to keep hold of the ball, passing it around to each other, everyone scrumming in for a touch, everyone doing their bit to waste a second for their lads. Eric took it upon himself to retrieve the ball, and, seeing it in the arms of a time-waster, gave an early outing of the Matthew Simmonds memorial drop-kick to release it. Except unlike the Simmonds, it was so perfectly timed the time-waster wasn't touched. Never-theless the Turk went down as if he had just encountered a Falls Road knee-capping squad. Eric, picking up the ball, turned and headed for the field as a diplomatic incident concocted itself in his wash.

But, extraordinary as it was, this was not the Eric moment that stuck in my mind from that trip. Nor was it the manner in which he made, with a single gesture, his contempt for the referee on the final whistle so abun-dantly clear that he was immediately shown the red card.

No, it was the morning of the match when we members of the press party were invited to the team hotel for a press conference. After Fergie's chat, we were shown round the former Sultan's palace which abutted the elegant riverside gaff where the boys were staying. While we were looking round the old Turkish baths, I spotted out of the window a sight which confirmed everything I had always hoped about Eric. Spurning the video library, unmoved by Robbo's crosswords, uninterested in Fergie's card school, Eric was passing the time before the big game on the balcony of his bedroom playing chess against Peter Schmeichel. And Schmeichel's body language, head in hands, groaning like Gary Neville had just scored a blinder of an own goal, suggested the King had him on the ropes.

Wilko

They usually prefix the Leeds manager's name with 'sergeant', but perhaps Regimental Sergeant-Major would be more accurate; should Alan Bennett ever write the tragi-comic Leeds story for the stage, Windsor Davies would surely play Howard. Such is the tabloid simplification anyway; to be fair, Wilkinson appears to be a touch more complex than his two-dimensional caricature. At least he has a sense of humour, thus marking him out as a dangerous maverick east of the Pennines ('Cantona . . . a natural room-mate for Batty, then' – arf!). During his first meeting with Eric in February '92, he sweet-talked him by using metaphors of love affairs, a clever tactic with any Frenchman and one that immensely amused Eric. In retrospect, how fitting was Wilko's pay-off line: 'Let's have a courtship that might end in marriage or Dear John . . .' There was indeed a marriage, but not at Elland Road; the 'Dear John' was not a letter, but a smoking fax from Eric in November asking for a separation. Wilko was to file this away in a safe as proof to the fans that it had been Eric, not the manager, who'd forced the break. I recall the Germans in 1939 citing our declaration of hostilities as evidence that we caused the war; as Basil Fawlty might remind us, what about the bleedin' invasion of Poland then?

Eric, as ever, has tried to be fair and generous in his assessment of a manager who seems to have later summoned up the ghosts of Tapie in Cantona's nightmares. He lavishes praise on Wilko for the way he built up Eric's self-esteem, for the force of his conviction that Eric could master the English game and for his willingness to dismiss past troubles and start with a clean credit record. By using the language of adventure and heroism, Wilkinson had led Eric to believe that a wholesale re-creation of the Leeds method based upon a central Cantona role was in the offing. At the end of the season, Wilko enthused: 'He's proved the most successful acquisition Leeds have made . . . he has presented a fresh new angle on our affairs', an interesting judgement given the later revisionism. When 1992/3 opened, Leeds were already attempting to play a more cultured, Cantona-friendly game which inspired some of Eric's best form, producing eleven goals. But the surface gloss concealed a flaking undercoat.

By November, Leeds's appalling away record had

already cost them a second title and their European challenge was dead. The Blackburn syndrome of post-title ennui had struck; too many players had lost the edge and were in danger of exposure as being unworthy champions in the first place. Neither the team, nor Wilko apparently, could escape the desire to retreat to the familiar, route oneish, direct blustering that had won the title in the first place; by merely tinkering at the edges, Leeds's management left Eric isolated. Where were the new players that they needed? Where was the public education that transformation takes time? And crucially, where was the personnel management skill to handle Eric in the right way?

Eric became the scapegoat for the Euro-exit and, some suggest, the target of those players who felt threatened by any prospective abandonment of their comfy but brainless direct play. 'Incidents' began to occur with frequent regularity between Wilko and Eric – a training ground snub here, a team hotel embarrassment there. Cantona's individualism now stood out in sharp uncomfortable relief where once it had been a welcome new dimension. The infamous team meeting bust-up which had provoked Wilko to send Eric home like the proverbial errant schoolie seemed a clear harbinger of crisis. The dark side of Eric was now on full view to all at Leeds; players speak of the unbearably tense atmosphere between a brooding Eric and growling manager. A last attempt at Maine Road to fit Eric in failed disastrously – a four-nil defeat. Chapman, left out that day, now crows that this was the moment Leeds had to realize that accommodating Eric was a mistake. Not a word, though, of the spineless performance of most of the other ten players, nor of the fact that Leeds have continued to be chronic under-achievers long after Eric's departure. Eric has since proved to be the best player in Britain when he is handled and used correctly, so who can blame Eric for refusing the blame offered to him by Chapman *et al* and instead fingering Wilko as the culprit?

The very words of accusation and recrimination that flowed between Eric and Wilko after the seismic sale on 26 November have become as familiar as those in any historic divorce. As with the parry and counter-thrusts of Chuck 'n' Di, enough ammunition was produced to keep the protagonists' apologists firing for the next five years. For Eric, the problems of 'decoding' Wilkinson's 'contradictory' language spoke most of all of that simplest divide: the personality clash, hidden at first when blind love is in bloom but exploding after a few months of pressurized co-habitation. Hey, we've all been there fellas. Lobbing in an extra incendiary grenade by suggesting Wilko had his own problems with popular players – Sheridan, Jones, perhaps now Brolin and Yeboah – was gratuitous and probably unfair but good dirty fun all the same. One thing is for sure amid all the crossfire: in the desperation to recoup the fee and perhaps in the desire to hand a rival a potentially soul-destroying, mercury-leaking personality, Wilkinson took an even greater gamble selling Eric to us than he had when buying him in the first place. What a loss, what a loser. (>> Anticipation)

Workmanship

Of all the insults and accusations thrown at Eric in the post-Selhurst maelstrom, perhaps the least appropriate was that Eric was 'unprofessional'. As even Howard Wilkinson concedes, no one could ever fault him for dedication to his craft, for the continued conscientious application to becoming a better professional. His profession also happens to be his art, but never has he used artistic licence as an excuse for dilettantism, unlike so many other self-proclaimed but inevitably under-achieving 'geniuses' in British football.

When he arrived at Old Trafford, he had to impress a man imbued with the Protestant work ethic who would never allow talent to excuse indolence. Within months, Ferguson was exalting Eric as an example to every pro when once he might have feared he had a typical workshy Continental artist on his hands. Cantona's application in training, not to mention his creation of extra technique sessions, is legendary. But the little things are symptomatic too, like still having the best body-fat ratio in the club despite being a gastronome – no chance here of a superstar letting the good life go too far as OT witnessed in the seventies and eighties with such depressing regularity. Again, he may have a Healeyesque 'hinterland' away from football yet he never forgets he is still a footballer even when off duty, maintaining an almost academician study programme of the latest technical and tactical developments from around the world in his spare time. Even when undergoing his community service punishment, he continued to take pride in his work, crafting a sophisticated regime for the kids and showing a commitment that impressed all who saw it.

At root, it is all about perfectionism, a phrase that occurs throughout Eric's own discourse on his art. 'Whatever happens, there are always things you could have done better. You score two and feel you could have scored a third. That's perfectionism, that's what makes you progress in life.' And the cause of perfectionism is pride; 'proud' is surely the first adjective one must use in describing Eric. As he points out, 'perfectionism is a need, it's not something you can teach. It's a question of character, of personal pride.' This, surely, is what elevates Eric above those past players who have claimed similar gifts and been fêted as geniuses. You know the players, that familiar list of hairy and hoary seventies heroes who now fill tabloid columns with their pathetic whinges, the ones who never got more than a handful of caps but who are lionized by the nostalgic footie press as the jack-the-lad gods. Where was their professionalism, their perfectionism, their pride when they were propping up bars or passing out in betting shops? Supremely skilled they may have been, but where was their urge to progress, to improve, to drive upwards? They cut such pitiable figures now because in a sense they had no pride. They let themselves down by not striving to fulfil their potential. And to those who see pride as one of the seven deadly sins, as a destructive selfish quality, think on. For those players also let down their clubs, their fans and the game itself; Eric's pride enriches, and is shared by, all of us around him.

'X' is for . . .

Xenophobia

'**A**ll wogs begin at Calais' – the maxim of the Little Englander throughout the centuries. Bad enough that Eric is foreign, but French as well? Nothing unites the English classes like suspicion of the French. After the Great War, the proletarian lions who survived the trenches came back full of grudging admiration for their German adversaries; it had been their French allies they couldn't stand. As for the donkey leadership class, there is no better illustrative quip than Sir Humphrey's to Jim Hacker: 'the British nuclear deterrent isn't to defend us from the Russians – it's to protect us from the French'. Cue uproarious guffaws from the bourgeois audience. Clearly, it takes more than the odd world war alliance to overcome the legacy of 900 years' animosity.

Long before the Selhurst Park conflagration, there was always a barely concealed dubious sub-text concerning Eric's Frenchness. Few writers could resist chucking in such stock phrases as 'French flair', 'typically Gallic', 'Continental temperament' and so forth. Amid praise, such slipshod generalization could be forgiven; when turned against him, these sentiments took on a rather less wholesome tone. Lawrie Sanchez's sneering, nationalistic attack on Eric after the Battle of Swindon was a sign of slurs to come.

Once Simmonds had been felled, that first public reaction – Lineker's pathetically unamusing 'he's lost *les marbles*' – carried the undertones that others would soon make explicit. Here was an example not merely of madness, but of French madness, not something our fair-play boys would stoop to but only to be expected from the garlic-crazed cross-Channel cowards. It is so much easier to pillory the outsider than one of your own – the domestic wrong-doer reflects on your own society but the foreign ne'er-do-well can be persecuted without shame or guilt. And as lynch-mobs down the ages have discovered, so much more effective if you can generalize some stereotypical assumptions about the minority that is your quarry. The 1930s Jew as money-grabbing parasite, the nineties Frenchman as violent lunatic – it's all the same majoritarian mindset.

The leader of *Red Attitude* once gently chided me, post-Galatasaray, for having a go at Turks in print, saying 'nationalist abuse is just a concealed form of racist abuse'. Politically correct? No: he was simply right. Anyone who understood how, post-Selhurst, the word 'French' became the most loaded, pejorative and frankly racist adjective when applied to Cantona can surely see that. Within days, *Red Attitude* and those of like mind began spreading the argument that the phrase 'French motherf*cker' does, in that context, contain *two* unacceptable descriptions. Official France soon followed suit: Philippe Piat, French players' leader, cited English xenophobia as bordering on racism, a line followed by much of the press and public. Remarkably, as even English opinion shifted uncomfortably in its seat, the understanding grew here too. The controversial but ground-breaking pairing of racial and nationalistic abuse made explicit by the Ferdinand/Cantona advert was the most visible example yet of England examining its insular mentality in the light of *l'affaire Cantona*.

Nonetheless, this is still a nation that places 'Hop Off You Frogs' next to 'Stick It Up Yer Junta' as its favourite headlines, where Cabinet Ministers routinely abuse Continental 'partners' in near-racist terms and whose glossy national footie mags still routinely refer to Keane as an 'Irish twat'. (Substitute 'Cole' for 'Keane' and 'black' for 'Irish' to see how unacceptable that is.) For the majority, nationalistic abuse remains an acceptable alternative for rightly suppressed unacceptable racist impulses, and I speak as one who admits to having fallen for the same sophistry. If the Cantona example has taught us one thing – and I hope the profile of Eric in this book bolsters the lesson – it is that every individual's genetic, racial and 'national' inheritance is so influentially overlaid by that individual's independent choices and existential action that mass generalization alone is useless as a character-study tool. In other words, racism sucks – and the correct penalty for shouting 'French motherf*cker' is indeed a boot in the chest.

XXX Appeal

The following is a wildly generalized and possibly insulting truism but it's probably true nonetheless. When it comes to United players' sex appeal with the girls, there are three stages of progression. For the teeny-boppers and pre-pubes, Ryan Giggs and David Beckham are the would-be main squeezes, up on bedroom walls next to Jason, Mark and Gary; 'safe' fantasies, both being too gentlemanly and boyish to be a serious threat to the hymen. By the late teens, they've moved on to Keano and Lee Sharpe – still the pretty-boy appeal of chiselled features and *Just Seventeen* smiles but surely more of a realistic carnal prospect. But for the fully fledged grown woman who has discovered the truth about both herself and men, there is only one sex god: Eric Cantona, a Real Man for Real Women. Just go and ask a few late-twenties female Reds for confirmation. Like the office-load of women who were asked by the *Evening News* what they'd buy if they won the lottery, the majority would reply 'Eric Cantona'. (The fact that a later poll in the same paper discovered 40 per cent of Mancunian men would prefer to holiday with Eric above any other person carries overtones that are best left unexplored.)

Surveying some female Cantonistas for explanations of this appeal unearthed the following comments: 'He's so dark, deep and brooding – the ultimate macho man'; 'He's the bit of rough who can give you a seeing-to then whisper poetry in your ear'; 'Strong, silent and masterful – he'd look after you'; 'It's the nose, know what I mean?' (?!?); 'If he treated you as sensitively as he does the ball, you could have no complaints'; and most root-level of all, 'I've heard he's hung like a horse.' Well really madam, so much for size not mattering.

That last response may have been prompted by the rumour that several frames from Eric's naked bathtime picture-shoot have escaped into public circulation which prove beyond all doubt that he needs more than a mere loofah to hide his back-scrubber, if you get my drift. The fact that he never consciously plays upon his sex appeal – you wouldn't catch him pulling doe-eyed poses like the front of Giggsy's book – only adds to the attraction. Nor has his supposed 'thuggery' put your average British woman off in the slightest. Looking at the popularity charts in the female press, from the teen glossies to *Cosmo*, Eric featured higher than ever in the months after Selhurst Park; in particular his alleged assault on Terry Lloyd, exhibiting the sort of primeval male instinct with which only Andrea Dworkin would find fault, has confirmed his status as a Real Man for the nineties.

Naturally, such a standing provokes every kind of sleazy mud-slinging imaginable. Both in France and later at Leeds, rumours have abounded of extra-curricular activity in the Ugandan department. If you believe the ridiculous stories Yorkshire Reds hear in the pubs, you'd conclude that the reason they all shag sheep over there is because Eric had taken all the women. It is said that none of it is true but it still adds a frisson to watching *Men Behaving Badly*, doesn't it?

'Y' is for . . .

Yorkshire

There's always one arse who claims to have been into something good before everyone else, isn't there? You know the drill: 'I saw the Pistols at the Free Trade in '76'; 'I got into the Roses when they were still neo-Goths'; 'I was wearing Lauren before the Brixton Boys' etc., etc. Here I have to admit to being one such smug twat: when I heard Eric was heading for Hillsborough in January '92, I'd already been a confirmed Cantonista since 1990; I started fantasizing about the possible routes that might yet bring him to Old Trafford. But never did I suspect that such a journey would be via the God-forsaken Elland Road; I suffered during those months of the Leeds–Eric love affair more than most.

Trevor Francis regularly appears these days as an 'expert' on Sky TV and in the tabloids, good going for a man who failed big-style at two Premiership clubs. He is, after all, the footballing equivalent of the Decca executive who turned down the Beatles after one audition in 1962. Asking a leading international who'd come recommended by such luminaries as Platini and Houllier – both with rather better track records than Trev – to trial

197

like some unproven sixteen-year-old naturally provoked nothing but disdain in Eric. At such a moment, a title was won and lost on the whim of an agent's dialling finger. Denis Roach is well connected at United; had we been a month further down the slippery slope of our '92 decline, perhaps Alex Ferguson would have been the lucky recipient of Roach's selling pitch. Instead, it was Sergeant Wilko (>>) who took the call to leave a tantalizing historical 'what if?' hanging in the air.

No Red wants to delve too deeply into the memories of that footballing Prague Spring, when life-long hopes were raised then shattered, so let us be brief. Eric played fifteen games of 1991/2 for Leeds, nine of them as sub; three goals and several assists resulted. It is now fashionable, as the Leeds regime attempts to airbrush Eric from the historical picture, to diminish the Cantona contribution, to make it appear that the final Trotskyite ice-pick in the head he received from Wilko was a matter of no great regret. But sod what Wilko, Chapman and the other revisionists might now say. The truest judges, without the festering personal jealousies that spin insiders' judgements, are the fans. This is hard for a Red to admit, but in truth both we and Cantona owe Leeds fans some credit for the influence they had on Eric. Within hours of Eric's first goal for them, he was a cult hero in the making; infamously, they stole our own 'Ooh-Ah Paul McGrath' that afternoon to pay initial homage. When Eric scored that stupendous ball-juggling third against Chelsea, the Tykes fêted him personally with a riotous gusto he never forgot. If some inside Sheep Central wouldn't admit it, the fans said it for them: Cantona's arrival had lifted the club and those around him to title-winning heights – moreover, he'd offered them the promise of superior quality for the future. It was Eric they singled out during those achingly painful title carnivals for the most intense worship, drawing from him that notorious 'I don't know why I love you . . .' soundbite. It is the fans' contemporaneous, wordless testimony that rings truest.

Obviously Eric's Yorkie intermission was important in pure football terms: he discovered he could master the English game. But then, as Platini had predicted, Eric was always one of the few Continentals who had the potential so to do. If you read what Eric says, even the most Flossy-f*cking-phobic Red must see that of even greater significance was the effect of the fans' worship on him. The proper committed English arenas inhabit an entirely different universe to those in France; the intense atmosphere and personal, passionate relationship a crowd here can have with a player were both entirely new and entirely entrancing for Eric. Even now that the sulphuric disenchantment between Eric and Elland Road is complete, he is still prepared to offer sincere public thanks to those Tykes who now despise him. Looking back to that time over the oceans of bile and venom in between, he still recognizes that they played the greatest part in his donation of heart and soul to the English game.

Of course, if you could measure love and devotion, the amount we Reds have lavished upon him since vastly overwhelms that with which he was smothered in Yorkshire. Leeds was the first, premature marriage that didn't work out: they are the Cynthias, we the Yokos (except that we're even less popular than the Jap screech-merchant.) However animalistic, indecent, violent and generally loathsome Leeds fans can be, at their best they are still capable of giving a prime demonstration of proper, unyielding, star-revering English supporterhood. Eric fell in love with that quality; we reaped the benefit from providing an even better version. So we too have cause to join Eric in a silent vote of thanks. Like Pacino and De Niro facing off in *Heat*, however much the Uniteds seek each other's blood, we recognize what we have in common – Manchester and Leeds are just the good and evil sides of the same supporting soul that bewitched Eric. That admitted, as Eric would've insisted, we can now return to trying to blow each other away. (>> Wilko)

Yuletide

Christmas has often been a traumatic time for Reds – any advance on 1978 for the very worst? – and even when it's been as good as it was in 1991 it has heralded not so much a 'New Dawn of the Saviour' but yet another crucifixion of our title hope come Easter. Xmas '92, however, truly did herald glad tidings to all Red-men. Jesus can keep the 25th; for us, the 26th would be the day to commemorate. A birth of sorts for our own 'Dieu' and a rebirth of Manchester United. That 3–3 chance-frenzy at Hillsborough had galvanized the team (>> Zapateado); Hughes, Fergie and others have all since looked back and pinpointed that day as the

moment champions were born. This time there would
be no rude hangover-strewn awakening on New Year's
Day – with Eric now fully tuned-up and ready to engage
his intellect as well as instinct, the Christmas festivities
were to be extended well into January. For the home
games with Coventry and Tottenham on 28 December
and 9 January have rightly passed into Old Trafford
legend. By the time the whistle blew on that latter 4–1
triumph, the team were not only on top of the League
at last but had alerted the world to two potent truths:
United were the complete team, Cantona the complete
footballer.

The doom-merchants, led by Cassandra Hansen, had
had much to spout on the subject of Eric and United,
but after the epochal 5–0 thrashing of Coventry any
remaining doubters had been smashed into submission.
Couldn't see how Eric would fit into the team? Thought
he wouldn't fancy the English winter? Didn't know if he
could handle pressure? Reckoned he was too selfish a
prima donna? On the darkest, coldest afternoon of the
season, Eric most certainly did fancy it – with relish.
When the pressure penalty came, he deputized for
Brucey to slot home with insouciance. Where lesser,
vainglorious men would've tried to snatch solo glory,
Eric stepped back to create for others in virtually every
goal movement. And as to where he would play, those
imbeciles hooked on old English creeds of fixed positions
and zones had their answer: wherever spirit, instinct and
vision took him. In short, wherever there was a link to
be made going forward, Eric could provide it. Whenever
imagination or originality was required, Eric would

invent it. And whoever sought service from a unique touch beyond normal capabilities, Eric could supply it.

Against Spurs, he had already demonstrated that he had mastered every striker's art; his deadlock-breaking goal meant that in a few games he had shown us the complete set of heading, shooting and dead-ball accuracy. But it was the fifty-first minute that produced a defining Cantona moment. His outrageous, visionary outside-foot stab for Denis to hammer home had Motson spurting all over his sheepskin and the Stretford End bursting out of their sodden pac-a-macs like dicks through johnnies. Eric had orchestrated these two demolition jobs and revealed his true footballing artist nature to us: the Creator-Destroyer. (>>Norwich)

'Z' is for . . .

Zapateado

(*. . . which is a kind of Spanish traditional dance involving a repetitive, rhythmic stamping of feet — and no, this is not about John Moncur's midriff.*) When League leaders Norwich turned up for their Old Trafford showdown on 12 December 1992, Fergie gave a good demonstration of what sets him apart from Wilkinson and his ilk. Had this been a task for play-safe Leeds, you can imagine where Eric would've ended up: on the bench or outside sorting kit à la Brolin. Alex bunged him straight into the team, 'relegated' Choccy to midfield thus settling Hughesie's nerves, and gave Eric his head. After only forty-five minutes of United footie and a couple of training sessions, Eric could hardly be expected to gel instantly with these strangers; for a mortal, it would've been asking for trouble. But Cantona is supremely equipped for the deep-end treatment. A man so self-reliant and confident in his own class doesn't need to have fully absorbed every foible of his team-mates and every nuance of his bosses' tactical plans to make an impact. For as we shall see, Eric's highest article of faith is to trust in his own instinct, to rely on spontaneity thus allowing his vision and skill to be expressed. You might prosaically dub this 'flying by the seat of one's pants'; few could do so with such poetic panache.

For this and the next two games, Eric was on a crash course of learning. If you looked at him off the ball, his eyes were darting everywhere, watching how his new colleagues moved, seeing how they meshed together, calculating his own geometry of pass and move with an architect's precision and an artist's vision. As a most serious student of the game, he must have revelled in the intellectual challenge; the result was that he appeared to have sussed United out, and formulated an ideal role for himself, in three games flat. Some have taken months, even years, to become so perfectly insinuated into a team. And the genius of it was that throughout the Norwich victory and the trips to Stamford and Hillsborough, he was no mere passenger being carried around a learning curve. Spontaneous instinct, subconscious even, allowed him to unfurl a series of his trademark classics – the feints, the flicks, the visionary passes, the cruising runs – and score two crucial goals, whilst his intellect busied itself with the lessons of United's ways. Apparently there are mountain-top mystics in Nepal who spend lifetimes trying to pull such a trick.

At Chelsea, right in front of the massed Red hordes, he rescued our Phelanesque performance with a supreme swivel-shot goal, dispelling any possible Birtles scenarios and sending those of us off to see Mozzer at the Pally with lighter hearts. But even that joyous terraced explosion was surpassed seven days later at Hillsborough. On a day when Reds took every end and thanked God for ever more that they'd been there, a sensational game drew a sensational fightback from the title-hungry United. If proof were needed that at last we had a striker with a touch of heavenly fortune about him, his eighty-fifth-minute equalizer provided it. Lunging at a cross from four yards, losing it, somehow reaching the rebound off a leg and scuffling the ball home . . . you can all admit that this was the best Christmas present you got that year. Eric then was that rarity – a player who is clearly as ecstatically delighted as the Red fans in front of him. Grasping his jersey as if in paroxysm, yelling some Gallic oath of joy towards the Leppings Lane frenzy, he danced the *zapateado* over to the hoardings to receive our tributes. He always was, as the song goes, 'poetry in motion'. *¡Olé!* (>> Yuletide)

Zodiac

Pretending for a moment that astrology is *not* a quack-driven scam for the gullible and insane, one can admit that Cantona is indeed an archetypal Gemini – artistic, restless, intellectual and, most importantly, contradictory. Like other famous Geminians such as Monroe, Kennedy and McCartney, it does sometimes appear that he has twin personalities within him. This book is about genius; my dictionary has a definition of genius as 'one of two opposed spirits or angels supposed to attend each person'. Perhaps in Eric's case we should have titled this an A to Z of Genii.

Cantona contradictions abound; some can be reconciled, some are left unexplained. He is a self-professed existentialist who is nevertheless happily in thrall to his childhood essence. He is a man of cultured artistic temperament who can cast aside the finer sensibilities if a kickin' bundle is in prospect. He is an eternal nomad who still craves the bosom of the family. He engages in prolonged reflective contemplation about life yet acts on a momentary instinct. He is in so many ways quintessentially French yet he has rejected that country to live within its opposite. It is an enduring problem for the Cantona student: pick up twenty Eric interviews and you could interpret him twenty different ways. Probably much of it is intentional on his part, like the 1960s Mick Jagger whose indefinability drove one critic to remark that he was 'weary from chasing his mysterious soul through the mazes of fun-house mirrors he had built to protect it'. Indeed, Eric has said, 'I don't want to be understood,' though you could probably find a quote that says precisely the opposite.

That is not to admit that every judgement in this book is mere guesswork and fanciful interpretation; I hope I've provided enough evidence to back what I've said and that you as a knowledgeable Cantona fan can take from it what rings true with what you have thought yourself. But the beauty of great personalities is that there can be so many ways of reading them; Ian Ridley, Richard Williams and myself have all had a go and we won't be the last. Only the banal and ordinary can be definitively encapsulated in one interpretation. Eric is special. He may be a man of contradiction and mystery but as Walt Whitman put it with a Cantonesque touch: 'I contradict myself? Very well, then: I contradict myself. I am large: I contain multitudes.' And few men in our Red lives loom as large as Eric Cantona. God save the King.

Epilogue:

May 11th 1996

Wembley Coach Park, about 5.30 p.m. Dozens of Reds down for the Cup Final on the infamous Burnage Boy Bus are reeling around the departing charabancs in frenzied celebration, both dazed and delirious. Twenty-four hours of intense substance abuse had played its part, of course – but the mainlining effect of Cantona's 85th minute winner topped anything they could snort or drink. 'The Curryman' approaches me, his dancing eyes testament to a night of John Belushi/Led Zeppelin behavioural impressions. Five seconds of lucidity intervenes: 'The only way it'll ever get any better than this,' he declares with a slur, 'is if Eric scores the winner in the European Cup Final.' In vino veritas, indeed: yes, it was that good.

Eric said precisely the same thing as 'The Curryman' next day. It had been a week of personal epiphany for Cantona already – Footballer of the Year one day, the news that he would become a father again next. (Some suggested that Eric should have shoved that award straight back up the orifice through which so many of the prize-givers talk but he contented himself with some entertaining toilet metaphors.) That he should display such technique, control and timing in scoring the goal that brought us the Double Double was, as he wryly remarked, ridiculously and cinematically glorious. Yet already he was looking to the future; just as Ferguson admits the moment of victory's delirium is fleeting, Eric had already focused on the greater challenge ahead. Because at Wembley, he and United had come full circle.

Just in terms of the 95/96 season, there is a pleasant circuity in Eric beginning and ending with personal triumphs against Liverpool. Back in October '95, Cantona was stepping into the unknown, a good ninety minutes that day no guarantor of future success and certainly no impediment to those on this back still betting on disaster and looking for the negative. By May, the transformation was complete, thanks to a self-imposed ban on tackling, decency from fellow pros and an instinctive self-preservation. Now the Cantona bandwagon groans under the weight of all who've clambered aboard to seek the reflected glory of Eric's successes and illuminate the positive. Eric says nothing, his actions on the pitch obviating any need to crow or gloat.

That Eric should score the Double Double winner, then lift the Cup itself, may well have been the fairy-tale that the cliché-mongers cite but it was also entirely logical and correct. Since he personally seized the initiative in late-winter, driven by all of the soul's demands which this book has discussed, he has in turn driven the team and Club forward to a triumph that few dared predict. The famous series of one-goal winners in itself was enough to grant him the title of Champion of Champions; add into the equation all that he created and the leadership he gave as a captain-elect and there can be no surprise in the overwhelming volume of votes he has received in every United player-of-the-year poll. The quality of some of his interventions has been astonishing, given the context. Earlier in this book, there is a Top Ten goals list: surely now his devastating blows against Spurs, Arsenal, Newcastle and Liverpool must be included in any such summary. Martin Edwards, ever the accountant, has remarked a touch prosaically on the twenty-one points Eric's goals directly won. But genius is unquantifiable. You can only make an approximate measure in terms of your feelings and emotional responses. They already called Eric 'Dieu' long before this season's final assault. Where are we going to find the words to express what he means to Reds now?

So: full circle – Wembley '94 to '96. Then as now, Eric's goals win the Double on the day, just reward for a season's dominance which has already been recognized by a Player of the Year trophy. Europe, and greater glories, await on the horizon. Last time around, a UEFA suspension, Romario 'n' Stoichkov and a combination of thug, authority and media conspired to drive the Cantona mission off the rails: now we're back on the grid again, in pole position. If Eric can continue to fly at his current elevated plateau for another season, then 'the Curryman' and Co. should book their liver transplants for May.

Appendix

SEASONAL SUMMARY

1992/93 Season

06.12.92	MAN CITY	W	2-1	7/10	

Second-half sub for Giggs

12.12.92	NORWICH	W	1-0	8/10	
19.12.92	Chelsea	D	1-1	8/10	Goal

6 yd swivel & shot on 71m to save point

26.12.92	Sheff Wed	D	3-3	8/10	Goal

2nd attempt scuffle on 85 to save point again

28.12.92	COVENTRY	W	5-0	9/10	Goal

65 min pen & made 2nd & 4th for MH & LS

05.01.93	BURY (FA)	W	2-0	7/10	
09.01.93	SPURS	W	4-1	9/10	Goal

Loop header on 40 to open; God-touch for DI on 51

27.01.93	NOTTS FOREST	W	2-0	8/10	

Made MH clincher on 68

30.01.93	Ipswich	L	1-2	7/10	

Set up Choc for fightback on 85

06.02.93	SHEFF UTD	W	2-1	8/10	Goal

Smash volley on 81; header to Choc for 1-1 on 64

08.02.93	Leeds	D	0-0	7/10	

Good gob-shot on full-time

20.02.93	SO'TON	W	2-1	6/10	
27.02.93	BORO	W	3-0	8/10	Goal

Danced through on paddock with 5 to go

14.03.93 ASTON V.   D   1-1   10/10

Set up MH header on 62; in fact, set up everything

20.03.93 Man City   D   1-1   8/10   Goal

Salmon-like leap for class headed point-saver on 68

24.03.93 ARSENAL   D   0-0   8/10

05.04.93 Norwich   W   3-1   10/10   Goal

Made Giggs' opener, finished for 3rd on 21

10.04.93 SHEFF WED   W   2-1   8/10

12.04.93 Coventry   W   1-0   7/10

Was refused pain-killer; subbed by Robbo

17.04.93 CHELSEA   W   3-0   9/10   Goal

Beat two close-in on 48 to head clinching 3rd

21.04.93 C. Palace   W   2-0   8/10

Crossed for MH on 64, set up Guv for 88m 2nd

03.05.93 BLACKBURN   W   3-1   8/10

Through-ball for Guv's 61st min party booster

09.05.93 Wimbledon   W   2-1   8/10

Sorted Fash with top piss-take

1992/3	pl.	gls.
League	22	9
FA Cup	1	-

Sucess Rates since August 1992:

Utd. with Eric	PL23	W16	D6	L1
Utd. Eric-less	PL27	W11	D8	L8

Success % with Eric: 82.61%

Success % without Eric: 55.56%

1993/94 Season

07.08.93	Arsenal (CS)	W	1-1*	7/10	
28.08.93	Southampton	W	3-1	9/10	Goal

Scored orgasmic 17th min chip from outside box

01.09.93	WEST HAM	W	3-0	9/10	Goal

Converted killer 44th min penalty

11.09.93	Chelsea	L	0-1	7/10	

17th min 40-yard lob hit bar; five yds better than Pelé

15.09.93	Honved (EC)	W	3-2	8/10	Goal

Knocked in simple 44th min third to put us in charge

19.09.93	ARSENAL	W	1-0	8/10	Goal

38th min free-kick harder and faster than Saturn 5?

25.09.93	SWINDON	W	4-2	9/10	Goal

Made opener then raced on for 40th min second

29.09.93	HONVED (EC)	W	2-1	8/10	
02.10.93	Sheff Wed	W	3-2	8/10	

Made Hughes' 66th min second to give us lead

16.10.93	SPURS	W	2-1	7/10	
20.10.93	GALASARAY (EC)	D	3-3	6/10	Goal

Bundled in 81m third to save proud home record

23.10.93	Everton	W	1-0	6/10	

Instigator of 53rd min winning goal move

30.10.93	QPR	W	2-1	8/10	Goal

35 yd rapier run & arrow shot for class 52m first

03.11.93	Galasaray (EC)	D	0-0	6/10	

90m wig-out, red card & police assault, oops

07.11.93	Man. City	W	3-2	10/10	Goals

Dropped deep yet slotted in on 52 & 78: classic EC

20.11.93	WIMBLEDON	W	3-1	8/10	

Made 65th & 80th goals for MH & AK

24.11.93	IPSWICH	D	0-0	8/10	
27.11.93	Coventry	W	1-0	8/10	Goal

Corner-flag pass sets up precise 60 min header

| 30.11.93 | Everton (LC) | W | 2-0 | 8/10 | |

Offside 'goal' & prime mover in clincher second

| 14.12.93 | NORWICH | D | 2-2 | 9/10 | |

Made 30 & 42 min goals plus funny hack at Canary

| 07.12.93 | Sheff Utd | W | 3-0 | 9/10 | Goal |

Fabulous third on 60m after 40 yd breakaway run

| 11.12.93 | Newcastle | D | 1-1 | 8/10 | |
| 19.12.93 | ASTON V. | W | 3-1 | 9/10 | Goals |

Swept in close on 22, made & finished 88m killer

| 26.12.93 | BLACKBURN | D | 1-1 | 7/10 | |
| 29.12.93 | Oldham | W | 5-2 | 9/10 | Goal |

19th min pen; made 4th & 53rd for AK & Giggs

| 01.01.94 | LEEDS | D | 0-0 | 7/10 | |

1st booking of season; what a savage hey?

| 04.01.94 | Liverpool | D | 3-3 | 7/10 | |

Pinpoint cross made Bruce's 9 min opener

| 09.01.94 | Sheff Utd (FA) | W | 1-0 | 7/10 | |

Joined fab interchange that made Hughes winner

| 12.01.94 | PLYMOUTH (LC) | D | 2-2 | 8/10 | Goal |

Close header on 60 smashed through keeper

| 15.01.94 | Spurs | W | 1-0 | 9/10 | |
| 22.01.94 | EVERTON | W | 1-0 | 9/10 | |

Hit post, missed sitter, Man of the Busby Match

| 26.01.94 | Portsmouth (LC) | W | 1-0 | 8/10 | |

Top cross made Choc's 28th min winner

| 30.01.94 | Norwich (FA) | W | 2-0 | 7/10 | Goal |

Funny 75m winner, booking and k-off with Polston

| 05.02.94 | QPR | W | 3-2 | 7/10 | Goal |

Far-post header on 44m to restore lead immediately

| 13.02.94 | SHEFF WED (LC) | W | 1-0 | 7/10 | |
| 20.02.94 | Wimbledon (FA) | W | 3-0 | 8/10 | Goal |

Unearthly 44th min touch & volley from 20yds

| 26.02.94 | West Ham | D | 2-2 | 7/10 | |
| 12.03.94 | CHARLTON (FA) | W | 3-1 | 7/10 | |

Set up AK for 71st min second

| 16.03.94 | SHEFF WED | W | 5-0 | 10/10 | Goals |

Set up MH smash; delicious box finishes on 45 & 55

| 19.03.94 | Swindon | D | 2-2 | 7/10 | |

Red card on 65 after stumbling onto Moncur's tum

| 22.03.94 | Arsenal | D | 2-2 | 7/10 | |

Made LS 2nd on 55; unjust 2nd card & off on 89

27.03.94	Aston V. (LC)	L	1-3	7/10	
30.03.94	LIVERPOOL	W	1-0	7/10	
23.04.94	MAN CITY	W	2-0	9/10	Goals

On 36 & 45: both close-in, both brill. Booked

| 27.04.94 | Leeds | W | 2-0 | 8/10 | |
| 01.05.94 | Ipswich | W | 2-1 | 8/10 | Goal |

Smart header down to level score on 36

| 04.05.94 | SO'TON | W | 2-0 | 8/10 | |

Set up MH smash, missed sitters

| 08.05.94 | COVENTRY | D | 0-0 | 8/10 | |
| 14.05.94 | Chelsea (FA) | W | 4-0 | 9/10 | Goals |

Double pens on 60 & 66 coolest ever?

1993/4	pl.	gls.
League	34	18
FA Cup	5	4
Lge Cup	5	1
Euro Cup	4	2

Sucess Rates since August 1992:

| Utd. with Eric | PL49 | W34 | D13 | L2 |
| Utd. Eric-less | PL14 | W8 | D2 | L4 |

Success % with Eric: 82.65%
Success % without Eric: 64.29%

14.08.94   Blackburn (CS)   W   2-0   8/10   Goal
Effortless 22nd min pen; knock-on for Guv goal

31.08.94   WIMBLEDON   W   3-0   9/10   Goal
Classicly headed 40th min opener

09.09.94   Leeds   L   1-2   7/10   Goal
74th min dodgy penalty; top piss-take of Palmer

17.09.94   LIVERPOOL   W   2-0   8/10
1-2 with Choc for 73rd min sealer; daft card on 87

24.09.94   Ipswich   L   2-3   7/10   Goal
Tap-in on 71m started fightback

01.10.94   EVERTON   W   2-0   8/10

15.10.94   WEST HAM   W   1-0   8/10   Goal
Amusing 5 yd tap-in after Martin pirouette

23.10.94   Blackburn   W   4-2   7/10   Goal
Levelling dodgy pen on 45 & set up AK on 82

29.10.94   NEWCASTLE   W   2-0   8/10

06.11.94   Aston Villa   W   2-1   7/10

10.11.94   MAN CITY   W   5-0   10/10   Goal
Blistering 24m opener; made 3 others & took piss

19.11.94   C. PALACE   W   3-0   8/10   Goal
Ghosted in to head clinching second on 37 mins

23.11.94   Goteborg (EC)   L   1-3   6/10
Made 64m equalizer; booked

26.11.94   Arsenal   D   0-0   7/10

03.12.94   NORWICH   W   1-0   9/10   Goal
Swept home from 12 yrds on 36m after Choc 1-2

07.12.94   GALASARAY (EC)   W   4-0   8/10
Instrumental in all but 1st goal; booked

17.12.94   NOTTS FOREST   L   1-2   8/10   Goal
Flicked on into net on 68m
26.12.94   Chelsea   W   3-2   8/10   Goal
46m pen, assisted winner & pathetic booking
28.12.94   LEICESTER   D   1-1   7/10
31.12.94   Southampton   D   2-2   8/10
Two superb crosses for goals on 51 & 79; booked
03.01.95   COVENTRY   W   2-0   8/10   Goal
Avenging 49m pen vs Pressley; set up opener on 29
09.01.95   Sheff Utd (FA)   W   2-0   8/10   Goal
Wondrous chip winner on 81; funny fight with #7
15.01.95   Newcastle   D   1-1   7/10
Missed late sitter
22.01.95   BLACKBURN   W   1-0   9/10   Goal
Inch-perfect 80th min header; booked
25.01.95   C. Palace   D   1-1   7/10
Unjust red card on 52; just kungfu kick on 54 . . .

1994/5   pl.   gls.
League   21   12
FA Cup   1   1
Eur Cup   2   –

Sucess Rates since August 1992:
Utd. with Eric   PL25   W16   D5   L4
Utd. Eric-less   PL34   W20   D8   L6
Success % with Eric: 74.00%
Success % without Eric: 70.59%

1995/96 Season

01.10.95 LIVERPOOL   D   2-2   8/10   Goal
1st min cross for Butt opener; 70th min pen & pole-vault

03.10.95 York (LC)   W   3-1   7/10
7th min cross for PS to start fightback

21.10.95 Chelsea   W   4-1   9/10
Made PS 2nd on 9m and dictated new 4-3-3

28.10.95 BORO   W   2-0   8/10
Made vital Cole relief goal on 87

04.11.95 Arsenal   L   0-1   7/10

18.11.95 SO'TON   W   4-1   8/10
Made 1st and 3rd inside 8 minutes

22.11.95 Coventry   W   4-0   8/10
Laid on Choc's 2nd on 76

27.11.95 Notts Forest   D   1-1   8/10   Goal
Match-saving pen on 66

02.12.95 CHELSEA   D   1-1   8/10
Booked for bugger-all

09.12.95 SHEFFIELD WED   D   2-2   8/10   Goals
Tremendous 17th & 83rd min finishes; carried team

17.12.95 Liverpool   L   0-2   6/10

24.12.95 Leeds   L   1-3   7/10

27.12.95 NEWCASTLE   W   2-0   8/10
Confirmed as King of France

30.12.95 QPR   W   2-1   8/10

01.01.96 Spurs   L   1-4   6/10

06.01.96 SUNDERLAND (FA)   D   2-2   7/10   Goal
Close-in header with 10 left to save season

13.01.96 ASTON VILLA   D   0-0   7/10
'Haircut, haircut . . .'

16.01.96	Sunderland (FA)	W	2-1	7/10	
22.01.96	West Ham	W	1-0	8/10	Goal

Close drive from acutest angle; birth of 'St Eric'

| 27.01.96 | Reading (FA) | W | 3-0 | 9/10 | Goal |

Easy last-minute icing

| 03.02.96 | Wimbledon | W | 4-2 | 9/10 | Goals |

Ducked on 70 to head 3rd; clinching pen on 80

| 10.02.96 | BLACKBURN | W | 1-0 | 8/10 | |

Through-ball to Cole led to LS winner

| 18.02.96 | MAN CITY (FA) | W | 2-1 | 8/10 | Goal |

Won & scored hilarious dodgy pen on 40

| 21.02.96 | EVERTON | W | 2-0 | 7/10 | |
| 25.02.96 | Bolton Wdrs | W | 6-0 | 6/10 | |

Carrying injury; subbed in 2nd half

| 04.03.96 | Newcastle | W | 1-0 | 8/10 | Goal |

50 min cross-box volley smashed into ground

| 11.03.96 | SO'TON (FA) | W | 2-0 | 8/10 | Goal |

50 min tap-in; danced through to set up 90m clincher

| 16.03.96 | QPR | D | 1-1 | 8/10 | Goal |

10 seconds left but time enough for genius header

| 20.03.96 | ARSENAL | W | 1-0 | 8/10 | Goal |

Sensational 25 yd chest & volley for 66m winner

| 24.03.96 | SPURS | W | 1-0 | 8/10 | Goal |

Superb 51m slalom and 25 yd pinpoint roller

| 31.03.96 | Chelsea FA | W | 2-1 | 9/10 | |
| 06.04.96 | Man City | W | 3-2 | 8/10 | Goal |

7th min pen, then feeder for AC & RG on 41 & 77

| 08.04.96 | COVENTRY | W | 1-0 | 8/10 | Goal |

Easy 7yd knock-in on 47 mins

13.04.96	Southampton	L	1-3	6/10	
17.04.96	LEEDS	W	1-0	7/10	
27.04.96	NOTTS FOREST	W	5-0	9/10	Goal

Blasted 89m icing after 30 yd run & 1-2 off NF tits

| 05.05.96 | Boro | W | 3-0 | 8/10 | |

Flicked-on for AC's title-clincher on 53

11.05.96   Liverpool FA   W   1-0   8/10   Goal
Technical marvel for 85m 18yd volleyed winner

Totals at time of going to press (16 March 1996):

1995/6	pl.	gls.		1992/6	pl.	gls.
League	30	14		League	107	53
FA Cup	7	5		FA Cup	14	10
Lge Cup	1	–		Lge Cup	6	1
				Eur Cup	6	2

Sucess Rates since August 1992:
Utd. with Eric   PL135   W92   D31   L12
Utd. Eric-less   PL86   W45   D21   L20
Success % with Eric: 79%
Success % without Eric: 65%